ONE DAY
A
THOUSAND
SONGS

Blue tit

To the world's forgotten soundscapes – and chickens!

It is May, the month of tenderness
Dylan Thomas, *Under Milkwood*

ONE DAY
A
THOUSAND
SONGS

John Miller

Merlin Unwin Books

First published in Great Britain by Merlin Unwin Books Ltd, 2026

Merlin Unwin Books
6 Rural Enterprise Centre
Eco Park Road
Ludlow
SY8 1FF
UK
www.merlinunwin.co.uk

ISBN 978 -1-913159-94-8
Typeset in 12pt Adobe Caslon Pro by Jo Dovey, Merlin Unwin Books
Printed by Bell & Bain Ltd, UK

CONTENTS

PART ONE

This story of a single day in a single garden in May, in Wiltshire, England, is not an ecological accident; it is the culmination of years of husbandry, weather patterns, and a reflection of the broader landscape and of springtime itself across the northern hemisphere. We will follow the circadian rhythm, the diurnal pattern that begins not quite with dawn, but with the silence just before it. The book is divided into six parts, each tracing that unfolding sequence throughout the day.

4:15 am

Quietly shutting the back door behind me, I am immediately struck by the sharp frost crisping the lawn – an unwelcome surprise for 6 May. Hardly the start I'd hoped for a marathon seventeen-hour day in the garden. A day set aside to see, hear and record each creature that shares our home – or each creature whose home we share.

I want to bring you the 'eighth wonder' of the world – the dawn chorus from the northern hemisphere.

The Location

The garden at Gypsy Furlong, Lockeridge, Wiltshire
We are fortunate to have a rich mix of mature trees, thick hedges, and patches of wildflowers – all managed entirely without chemicals.

John Miller, May 2026

Robin

DAWN
The Morning Fanfare

♪ **04:35**

And so it starts. One tiny, solitary note, awkwardly and nervously at first, but with the temerity to defy the astronomical hour, attempting to hurry the dawn forward. And then another, and another, until an imagined spiral emerges, metamorphosing into melody. Nature's alarm clock stirs slowly, deliberately, and gradually.

For I am a bold **robin** with two big eyes who can see pretty well in the dark. I come from the tangled forests of fairy tales and Ents. I followed the wild boars and foraged in their leaf litter, adding to folklore – 'the early bird catches the worm.' Now, I follow man into the vicinity of workplace and homes as the weather turns and the nights chill – and for this, you paint me on your Christmas cards.

A diffident, domineering, pugnacious bird, friends with no others, safe in his proximity to man. To see one now in a wildwood seems out of place – a surprising incongruity lost in time. Perhaps that is why it lives this hour with the stage to itself before the blackcap or garden warbler competes for the airwaves.

It lifts the dawn gently while we talk in muffled tones, trying not to intrude. Like an entertainer with an appreciative audience, his song feeds his confidence, and the notes become bolder. The rustling leaves in the light breeze, indeed, all the white noise of the wind dims to listen to the maestro. No wonder the nursery rhyme *Who Killed Cock Robin?* is so enduring.

'Who killed Cock Robin?
I said the Sparrow,
With my bow and arrow,
I killed Cock Robin.'

One bird is guilty, but the need for reparations and amends rallies all the local creatures – an owl, linnet, lark, fish, dove, kite, wren, thrush, bull, and beetle – all collectively seeking partial atonement.

'And all the birds of the air,
Fell sighing and a sobbin'
When they heard the bell toll for poor Cock-Robin.'

I think I know this robin who raised a brood earlier in the year. It was a typical robin's nest, safely tucked away inside the mower shed, behind a washing line that had been put away for the winter. The neat little cup of moss, lined with hair, contrasts with the sprawling mass of dried leaves that formed the robin's typical, untidy foundation. His mate laid five eggs, each a pale, almost translucent white with streaks of reddish blotches as if coloured by her own red breast. From the nest, her fixed eye looked deep inside my reassuring company, an acceptance rare in animals. We warm to her fearlessness in our company and take her to our hearts. Not so the pigs and goats, who boldly clock you, with their unnerving eye, making life a little uneasy.

The robins know they are safe in our presence, and they act like a bolder bird about the place, constantly darting in and out of cover, but happier in the open than, say, the dunnock or wren. They have their favoured outpost, maybe a wall or fence, or the classic fork stuck in the kitchen garden, from which to dive on some tasty morsel, never venturing too far away from shelter.

He commands a territory in the middle of the garden, including the productive (for him) vegetable patch, while a second pair lives down by the compost heap, and finally, a third pair lives in the front garden. This last pair is sitting on eggs, sheltered from the westerly rain and northern wind in the twisted stems of honeysuckle clambering up the outside wall by the front door. Another mass of messy leaves harbouring a deceptively neat cup of fine hairs, roots, and moss to cocoon the eggs.

♪ **04:36**

Almost immediately, only a minute later, a **blackbird**, encouraged by the smaller robin, softly pipes his flute before repeating the same lines louder each time until the two birds compete full on. This is what the dawn chorus is all about.

There is a wistfulness to the blackbird's song – a fluty melody rich in thoughtful notes – the garden's finest and most consistent songster.

He straddles, high, the top branch of a small tree – a 'blackbird in a pear tree', a dark, opaque music box, among a cluster of leaves – their green just visible in the emerging sky. Within earshot, his mate warms her clutch of four mottled olive eggs; he is free to sing loudly again, confidently, in tune and volume, taking centre stage over the early robin.

There is a story to this bird: with his mate, he built a nest behind The Shed, back in March, and together they successfully fledged four young by 19 April. In the dry spring, they scoured my kitchen garden in the damp compost, scattering it across the paths – a small price to pay as they sought out the snails, slugs, and their eggs. In May, and unusually for blackbirds or any other songbirds, they raised another brood in the same nest. By June, the fledglings were following their parents around the garden. 'Feed me, feed me,' they demanded. After two broods, the nest was a mere platform of matted, deadened grasses mushed up by tiny feet, encrusted with their excrement.

To my astonishment, the mother laid a third clutch of four eggs in July, without any attempt to bolster the nest. On 29 July, without the safety of a proper home, the inevitable happened when I had to pick a baby off the ground and put it back on the platform. An eye bulging, naked chick, flailing its tiny wings tipped with ink as the pinions pushed their way through to freedom. Only pigeons and doves nest with such fragile faith, but then they only ever nurture two siblings at a time.

♪ **04:37**

In the background, the **wood pigeons** are feebly cooing, the **jackdaws** nearly '*daw, daw*', and a **pheasant** cries a half-hearted, single note. 'We are here but not yet ready to make an effort.' They are stirring, but unlike us, they have no commute ahead of them. So what is going through their heads? Will the car start, or will the train be on time? Is the water hot for a shower? No need to run through prep once more for meetings. No need to plan the week – no arguments to win. Just wake up, preen your feathers, and find some food or a mate – simple. But don't get nabbed by a passing hawk, and oh, watch yourself on the ground for foxes and cats. Simple, but life and death are never far away.

Sing while you can, and don't spend energy unnecessarily.

Being fully diurnal birds, pigeons will not leave their roost, wasting calories while their faculties are still dimmed. Their excellent eyesight, rich in colour perception, equips them perfectly for feeding – but only once daylight strengthens. So, they sit, chatter, and wait, while the robin, on the other hand can cope with a touch of dimness. Along with the blackbird, it is therefore among the first to rise and the last to retire.

The early bird catches the worm…

In winter, as the day slowly creeps back, look up through the bare trees. Blurred smudges cling to last night's roosts as minute by minute, the smudge becomes woodpigeon. I marvel at how they cling to the same slender branch where they settled the previous evening, having hung out all night in the blowy, cluttery weather. They seem in no hurry to start their day.

As a small boy, I clearly took the nursery rhyme Who Killed Cock Robin? *to heart, although the picture shows my frustration in being given a bow and arrow with harmless red suckers on the ends of the arrows – it still rankles sixty years later.*

♪ **04:38**

Old 'Nog' the **heron** – named after the character in Henry Williamson's *Tarka the Otter* – announces himself with a single, hoarse *'Kraak'* from across the paddock by the river. I imagine there's good feeding there just now, with water levels dropping rapidly after the dry spring, young trout left stranded in the shallows. Which reminds me, I really must take a look.

> *On 18 June last year, I walked among the boulders, pots and gravels of the drying river at the end of my garden, disturbing two well-fed herons. I panicked a shoal of trout trapped in the belly of warm, algae-saturated water. The sun sucked out the last vestiges of oxygen, as flies swarmed over the newly emerged mud, revelling in its foul, stinking putrefaction. The trout darted in every direction, the largest easily respectable at a pound and a half. Frozen at the water's edge, like Nog, I pressed myself into the grasses, but instead of spearing the fish, I felt for their predicament, willing them to settle, to find calm amidst the turmoil.*
>
> *No route upstream, no route downstream – panic! This was made even sadder by the many thousands of stickleback fry and the odd bullhead littering the shoreline in a silver glimmer. We returned two days later with nets and buckets to at least save the trout, too late to save their smaller brethren.*

Herons are usually early risers. This one's too wary to venture into the garden, but come September, we often see the year's young making a bold inspection of the pond. Never judge a book by the cover, because these adolescents, all wings and legs, wrapped in a bundle of feathers, have a steely look and a beak to match. Anything goes, vole, mouse, rat, or duckling if fish are scarce. They are opportunistic survivors.

♪ 04:40

From the same direction, a **rabbit** lets out a hysterical scream, its life draining away, run down by a **stoat**. And, as if to command sole monopoly for primordial sounds, a dog **fox** barks from Stanley Copse. The stoat had better finish his meal sharpish – the fox would recognise that scream for what it was: an opportunity.

♪ 04:50

I wonder how long the **blackcap** has been waiting for this moment as, at 4:50, fifteen minutes after the robin, he joins the show, a hesitant start before he clears his throat and lets out a long, fluid song from the wild cherry tree.

His place is here each year, among the flowering cherry blossoms – their white sprays scattered randomly along the branches, before one by one the wind blows single petals down – white confetti on the grass below. He sings in short bursts, then flits down from the canopy into the understorey of the more structured hazel stool.

Distinct from the carefree cherry, the hazel is disciplined: each bud set in perfect symmetry, opposite its twin, at standard, regular three-inch intervals. From every node emerge three leaves of freshest green, while the smaller, vestigial bud-bursts linger pale and redundant.

And then the blackcap flies up to the maligned sycamore, a tree cast out as a non-native. But it plays a valuable role in attracting a multitude of insects, which are picked off here in the garden by blackcaps, dunnocks, chaffinches, chiffchaffs, and blue tits. Who are we to assign value based on an ideological whim when nature is so dynamic?

I remember May last year in Cornwall, the wettest rain (Cornish rain) persisting through our wettest man-made skins, and there under one tree, and one tree only, were half a dozen swallows finding insects in that one place – the sanctuary of a sycamore tree.

This scruffy, untidy area of the garden always attracts the first blackcaps of the year, a neat, smart grey bird with a sooty black cap, confidently singing in these emergent trees. An energetic, outstanding, bubbling joy of a song – quickly called out – '*hee-ti-weeto-weeto*' – before he moves to another branch, while you struggle to put sound to sight. He is not shy, just overexuberant, seemingly just above your head, with such loud notes, but where? Finally revealing himself as he darts out of the twigs to snatch a passing fly. I don't remember them as a child, but here in Wiltshire, they must be our most common warbler, along with the chiffchaff.

He was late this year, on 25 April, but listen out if you hear a melody in your garden, which is not a blackbird. It is probably a blackcap, sometimes called the 'northern nightingale', particularly tuneful, slightly bolder, and as heartwarming as his namesake, as he stakes out his territory before the returning females, which in contrast have a chestnut brown cap on top of their heads.

Where the nettles and cow parsley climb tall, giving the cleavers a helping hand up into the lower branches of shrubs and hedges, the blackcap make their nest. It is not such a neat nest as others, being a collection of dried grasses, often only two or three feet off the ground. After the snowdrops have bloomed, I leave this corner undisturbed until midsummer, and when the surge of spring growth has ceased and dried under the trees, I look for the disused blackcap nest. No coincidence, it is in the same place the muntjac hides her young like a hare, only returning quietly to feed in the early evening.

♪ 04:51

A **carrion crow** signals a single caw by the river. The dark devil is astir; his black beak, his weapon of choice, will send a shiver somewhere, to some creature, before the day is done. The cock pheasant crows again, letting the hens know he is awake.

♪ 05:00

Bold and brash, a **wren** with his cocky, stumpy tail angled skywards, trills louder than all the other birds, many times his size. I was beginning to feel irritated by his relentless song, drowning out everything else. This tiny king of a bird, as the old fable tells, flew higher than the eagle by hiding beneath its wing before darting out, just as the eagle proclaimed he could fly higher than any other creature.

And then, the wren landed – just three yards in front of me – striking that classic songbird pose, beak wide open, letting it rip. He must have been at full volume; there was nothing more to give. And yet he shimmered – shimmered with wings stretched out and fluttering in a provocative, flirty display.

The wren is always on the move, playing hide and seek with your eyes – a mouse in your peripheral vision or, more accurately, the hustle and bustle of a shrew – too busy, too fast to stop and talk, but then he did just that – he suddenly stopped, and that's what made it so special.

His song follows his jerky movements, an uneven blend of notes he fires out rapidly to the world in quick succession. 'Listen, everyone, this is important.' Then he abruptly stops, goes to find food, his hyperactivity getting the better of him.

When alarmed, and if you approach his nest, a sprawling mass of dead leaves and moss but with a neat entrance hole, the wren will scold you with a rapid *'tic-tic-tic'* warning. In the winter, I see them diving into great grassy tussocks by the river, where insects and their larvae shelter from the elements. In the garden, untouched clumps of herbaceous flowers serve the same purpose – another reason for a little less gardening tidiness.

♪ 05:02

Where the garden meets the meadow and falls away to the River Kennet, a drunken line of molehills wends out from the trees, under the fence, and into the field. Each is a mini volcano, sparkling white with this spring frost, save for two smaller crumbly mounds still fresh and brown. It looks like steam rising from the inside. They were thrown up this morning, the warmer soil warding off any frost. It is rare to see moles at work. They must have felt my approaching steps and fallen silent in their digging.

It is July when you are most likely to actually see moles – youngsters striking out from the family home to find new territories of their own. Then you can marvel at the little gentleman – or lady – clad in soft, grey-charcoal fur, with pink hands far too large for such a tiny body. Their sleek fur, like velvet, has no natural lie or grain as the mole moves easily forward, backward, and sideways in long tunnels under the grass.

This is when they often make shallow runs or break clean out onto the surface of the lawn. But then, like ducklings struggling to dive underwater with their buoyant fluff, these young moles wrestle to break back underground again, to go back into the earth below to safety and the steady supply of earthworms they must find each day. Emerging from their underworld, their tiny eyes uncomprehending, they are suddenly vulnerable, exposed to the unforgiving glare of daylight. Many will fall to buzzards; others will be reduced to playthings for cats.

♪ 05:04

The first **goldfinch** piped up just after 5am. In this garden, that means a continuous twitter will carry on through the day – the sound of our most familiar bird, present all year round. I know of three active nests tucked into the creepers on the house, though I am certain there are more hidden elsewhere.

Amongst all the gloom of disappearing birds, this is another success story, perhaps helped by winter bird tables, and so many ready-made nesting opportunities among our garden shrubs, orchards, and small trees.

The nest is exquisite – the neatest cup of moss, roots, and grass decorated on the outside with lichen and inside, a sheltered cocoon of horse hair and feathers. Once the brood near fledgling, however, they are not shy in 'messing' their own bed, and by the time the young fly, often all that remains is a dried conglomeration of lichen and bird droppings on a well-trampled platform, as the nest loses its shape.

You can understand why they were such a popular caged bird in Victorian times, since they bring happiness to the garden, and unlike the robin and the wren, they revel in each other's company. The trade in birds captured, particularly on the South Downs, sadly ran into the tens of thousands each year. However, with no internet, Spotify, iTunes, discs, tapes, or radio, you can imagine how their presence once brightened the drab, dark city dwellings of yore, connecting society back to the countryside. Even as a boy, a goldfinch was a rare sight, so God bless them, here now in Wiltshire.

 *Later in the year, they twinkle among the wildflowers, their red faces momentarily lost in the poppies, and their yellow wing bars match the corn marigolds as they pick the seeds from the contrasting sky blue cornflowers.*

♪ **05:12**

Looking west, the dawn still silhouettes the trees, but turn your gaze east, and colour seeps back. The chestnut candles, pale blobs at first, begin to turn white proudly in their cradles of spring green.

The monotone of night gives way to the heavenly spectrums of light, returning to settle the gaze. It is in these heights we search the source of music. You must filter through the constant background chittering of goldfinches, the '*daw daw*' of the jackdaws and the welcoming pigeons cooing to each other, until somewhere above, a singular song cuts through the ensemble, distinct in sound as in species.

A **chaffinch** has pitched in with his particularly loud, somewhat monotone, insistent refrain: '*will-you will-you will-you will-you will-you will-you*'.

Meanwhile, the female is a little more industrious, foraging among the sycamore flowers, ferrying food to her newly fledged brood scattered among the lilac bush, holly and a yew hedge. They keep low, tucked in the base where a thick tangle of cow parsley protects them from prying eyes.

One alarm call from her, and they will instantly stop calling and go quiet to await the all-clear. '*Don't put all your eggs in one basket*' must be etched into their instincts. Follow your siblings out of the nest quickly, or risk being the last one the stoat finds. But once out, scatter, each taking a different path.

It is easy to become complacent with our more common birds and overlook the male chaffinch singing in May. He is beautifully dressed in every shade of pink to rose red in the best sunlight, set off by his striking white wing bars.

In comparison, the fledglings are pale imitations of their drab mother, designed to blend into the herbage, with stumpy wings and short tails, calling softly for food. I never did find their nest, though I knew it was nearby. When the leaves fall and winter flattens the exuberance of spring's growth, I'll try to find the home they left behind – somewhere below where the blackcap attempted to teach their father to move on from singing nursery rhymes.

♪ **05:14**

A **rook** passes over with a solitary *'caw'*, the first of many flying out from the small rookery stacked up in the Scots pine trees by the village Primary School. They will forage all day, black specks among the sheep on the Downs, tacking back wind-blown and waving like sheep paths in the sky to feed their young. They rarely venture into the garden, except nest building, when a particular twig has caught their eye.

Rooks never appear to be in a hurry or flustered, tolerating the many noisy and squabbling jackdaws who always accompany them. They are a bird of 'place', and when one December a neighbour removed the nests, and significantly reduced the breadth of the Scots pines, they still returned the following February. The trees have grown back twice as risilient, and the colony is as strong as ever.

♪ 05:15

A **great tit** revs up its *'tee-chu tee-chu'* phrase, commonly known as 'teacher, teacher', in the holly tree. They are nesting in a box next door against a wall, and he will soon be too busy collecting food to waste energy singing, as the chorus begins to fade away. That nest box had a wasp nest in it last year, and I would love to know how the birds approached it as a 'des res' this spring. It must have been quite an effort to remove all the now-disused grey paper comb.

As spring and summer progress, the Great tits become adept at finding insects in the blooms of large flowers, especially the buddleia species and the purple Jerusalem artichoke thistles. They will even take butterflies if they catch them napping. As they hunt the garden, their sharp focus indicates an intelligence beyond the blue tits' random searches.

♪ 05:16

Up to now, the **jackdaws** who nest in a loose colony of about twenty pairs in the epicormic shoots of the lime trees at the bottom of the garden have been arguing in their nuisance way; they talk in their sleep, complete insomniacs, but only now venture out to seek breakfast.

They speak with the bleating lambs – a constant backdrop to the night. I once set about clearing the mass of epicormic shoots from one of the six lime trees, but after finding multiple mummified baby jackdaws, addled eggs, dead bats, and the like, I thought I would leave it to the wildlife. Besides, it would only grow stronger and require cutting on an annual basis. We have an unwritten law that jackdaws stay away from the house, where birds can nest in peace, and stick to their own part of the garden.

The tawny owls and buzzards, in turn, terrorise the jackdaw nests when they want a change from voles and mice – good luck to them, especially the owls, who can wake me up anytime.

♪ 05:26

Now here is one of the great songsters. At last. I have been waiting for him all morning.

The **song thrush** is one of the most straightforward bird calls to recognise. He struts out a precise three-note, melodious song like a child on a recorder – it's not complex, it's ready-made, with the repetition of three notes easily put into onomatopoeia, hence the old English name of 'thrice cock'.

'Did he do it?, Did he do it?, Did he do it?
He did! He did! He did!
Phew, phew phew.'

A song for the moment, when the world is still looking forward to the day ahead. He always seems so pleased to sing, like a human in a choir, for the love of the sound. He is not squirreled away in a bush like a nightingale but proudly front and centre stage, enjoying himself in the brightening sky. Perhaps today we will hear his 'tap tap' as he uses a stone or concrete path as an anvil to break open a snail.

We have such an anvil, a big lump of our local sarsen stone, regularly used in the herbaceous border. The same stuff that has kept Stonehenge standing for millennia. Scattered amongst its moss and the surrounding earth are many broken shells – the remnants of snails. These are not big fat garden snails, but brown-lipped snails, so called for their brown banding around the opening of the shell. They have an array of different colours, from red, brown and pink, and are seemingly harmless in the garden. I leave them for the thrushes.

A slight breeze picks up the trees; perhaps the sound is their new-found green canopy, soft in its youth, free to flow with the breeze, rustling across the garden. Each tree has its distinct spring colour, before the sun and droughts of summer merge all the verdancy as one.

♪ **05:30**

Within this richness, another bird demands attention. The **mistle thrush** sings as if he were in the next county, his song blowing in the wind, somewhere out where the rainbow arcs – a place you will never find. I have always found it strange for a bird to proclaim its territory from afar. It is short, loud, and fluty.

And then, from nowhere, he appears in that looping woodpecker-like flight before alighting in his chosen tree, before running along the branch, coyly stopping on his way to his nest.

I am not aware of any other bird that exhibits quite this distracting behaviour. He is confident but wary, and woe betide any passing squirrel or magpie, for he will launch an attack with much noise and aggression – part of the reason I like having them in the garden. His '*churring*' attacks are like the sound made by violently shaking a wooden rattle, if you can remember your *Beano* comic; this is noise, not music, but very effective. His pugnacity is not restricted to predators, and woe betide any blackbird or chaffinch that crosses an invisible boundary close to his nest.

There is a distinct difference in mistle thrush decibels between the presence of a songbird close to its nest, such as the amiable wood pigeon, or even a far off predator seventy-seven yards away. But if the threat level rises and a predator moves closer, the noise brings me running from the house. I have watched them drive a squirrel out of their tree and follow up across the lawn to make sure it will never dare return.

As usual, the mistle thrushes started nesting in our big larch tree in March, only to be booted out of their first home by a pair of amorous pigeons. They then tried nesting a little lower in the same tree and abandoned that for some reason. Now somewhat late, they have rebuilt in earnest in another larch tree. (By the way, grow larch trees just for the mistle thrushes – they love them.)

I watched them snapping off pliable birch twigs to form a foundation for a home with a 360-degree view, hidden from above by the emerging larch needles. Still, they mysteriously abandoned that nest too and finally settled for a spot two-thirds up a copper beech tree at a fork in the main branches. It was not until 16 April that the hen finally began incubating, which is late for our mistle thrushes. She sits there, with her mate guarding their hinterland, and I can only assume that she wanted somewhere with bare branches, while she incubates, with a good view of any impending danger, since the larch tree needles are now out in their sporty green.

Disaster occurred three days later, on 19 April, when one of the buzzards who liked to sit in the very same copper beech tree finally saw through the tragedy of the thrushes' defensive bluster and took out the nest. For the next two days, I did not see a mistle thrush in the garden and presumed (somewhat sadly) that they had given up breeding for the year and left the neighbourhood.

To my surprise, on 22 April, they were back and rebuilding the second nest they had previously abandoned. Three nest attempts in three different trees – determination – they like our garden. It seems to me that the female does most of the nest building while the cock bird keeps guard, watching over proceedings. I expect that is the last song I will hear from him this year until December, since they are not part of the dawn chorus, expending all their energy on being the garden vigilantes.

Mistle thrushes usually nest relatively high up, so it's not often we get to see their eggs. A few years back, a pair built a nest only six feet off the ground which, in hindsight, was a bad idea since it was raided. However, it did give me the chance to look at the eggs. They resemble a large song thrush egg, but are an unusual, chalky, milky pink with darker blotches instead of the deep blue of the song thrush.

♪ **05:38**

Now here is a strange song, which I am sure catches people out – the overlooked **stock dove**. Quite the opposite of a mistle thrush, it is a sound of 'place', breeding among the jackdaws in the tangled mass of lime epicormic. Wherever you see ancient lime trees in parkland settings, you will likely find stock doves. They are such pretty birds – smaller and slimmer than wood pigeons, with black wing bars. In place of the pigeons' white neck ring, they have a stunning mix of irridescent green and purple, which shimmers in the sunlight, beautifully contrasted with the soft grey feathers of the neck and head. Their black wing bars are distinct when flying, and for identification, they do not have the rock doves' white rump.

When William Wordsworth wrote *The Nightingale and the Stock Dove*, he called it a 'murmur of delight,' evoking peace and contentment, contrasted with the nightingale's lovelorn sense of longing and passion. I will take murmur and delight at the end of the garden as I look out across the Kennet valley on a May dawn any day. However, the urgency and echoing *'woo, woo, woo'* has a persistence that goes way beyond a simple murmur. I feel that description is more apt when the sound is muted by hedges and grasses far away across the fields.

♪ **05:40**

A male **spotted flycatcher** calls from the top of our tallest hawthorn tree, now heavy with blossom. He's calling for a mate. The male typically arrives first each spring; this year, he was especially early. I first heard his rasping song on 30 April. His mate – or at least, a female – returned on 11 May, which is also historically early. They don't waste time; by 20 May, she was already sitting on eggs. Blink, and they are sitting on eggs often before you even realise they have returned.

The hawthorn typically blooms in May, hence its common name 'May tree' and 'May blossom', even if climate change is bringing this date forward. However, now, in May 2025, it is still at peak blossom with its creamy-white flowers escaping out of the garden into the valley, a colourful ribbon along the river Kennet and beyond, across the landscape up onto the Downs. It is as much a part of the countryside in May as the dawn chorus.

♪ **05:42**

The **blue tits** are too busy to sing these days, with a family nestled in an artificial house martin box outside my office window, and only now emerge to search for food. They are the most diligent of parents in gathering caterpillars, due to their large broods. Today, they return individually to the nest about every three minutes. However, later in May, I watched one parent bring a caterpillar back three times in under a minute, from a plum tree. I went to said tree to check for an infestation, but I couldn't find even a single aphid! If I open my office window, I am met with a sharp scolding *'chee, chee, chee'*, and the young stop bobbing their heads around the nest hole and slink back out of sight.

There were many blue tits in the garden all winter, not surprising with the mild winter, but for some reason, that does not appear to have continued into the nesting season. Although we have had plenty of sunshine in this dry spring, the nights have remained cold, and this may have reduced the abundance of insects.

♪ **05:44**

Like the chaffinch, the male **greenfinch** enjoys singing most of his time, often throughout the entire day. He is now pushing out his long, repeated *'tswee-twsee-twsee-twseeeese'*, described as a wheeze. Although it's now only May, he is one of the few birds to continue this song throughout the summer, even on hot days when he will be the only songbird still in tune.

I first found this pair's nest back in April, when I watched an adult greenfinch pick up a pigeon feather; there are always many scattered across the lawn – and I followed her flight to the nest. It was a textbook example: about twelve feet up, tucked into the edge of a yew hedge, beautifully lined with horsehair and feathers. Unfortunately, just a week later, I had the misfortune of witnessing a magpie stage a classic 'smash and grab' on the eggs.

It was not until early July that I found a second greenfinch nest. Again, it was near the top of another beech hedge, wedged into the crook of a spindly yew growing up through the centre. It lacked the neatness of the chaffinch and goldfinch, with a feather cup nestled on a broader platform of grasses, roots and small twigs bound together with moss. Five eggs – a dirty white with light reddish-brown speckles at the round end, but two distinctly stained, darker, or grubby as you would describe a child's face. I took a note, and when the young had fledged a few weeks later, climbing up the ladder for a peek, two addled eggs remained. Song birds nearly always make a new nest for each clutch, but perhaps in this case, the female had been caught short, so she had made use of an old nest.

Little bands of young goldfinch will stay around all summer with their constant 'chi, chi, chi'. The greenfinch on the other hand sounds a bit like 'chipper chipper'.

♪ 05:45

Almost on cue, a **magpie** 'chatters' in the garden and immediately flies off upon seeing me. Keep flying and don't come back.

♪ 05:54

Every now and then, I can just about make out a **treecreeper** singing somewhere high up in the lime trees at the front of the house. It is a complex sound to pick out – high-pitched and intermittent, easily overlooked. Of all the birds in the garden, the Merlin bird app shines here, as the treecreeper is easy to spot at ground level on a tree trunk, but it's a different story when they're 'doing their thing' high up in the canopy.

And 'doing their thing' means pretending to be a mouse as they creep along the bark, with their pointy, probing beak. They breed in the garden every year, yet their nests remain elusive. They occupy a distinct niche, foraging almost exclusively by moving inconspicuously along tree trunks in search of insects and spiders. Flying down to the base of the trunk, they begin another silent ascent, quietly probing the bark with their thin, pointed beak.

♪ 05:55

Next into view – and song – is the **dunnock**, or **hedge sparrow,** as we called them in our childhood. In the lower branches of a birch tree ahead, three of these usually shy birds are doing some dance: two males vying for the attention of a female who already has a nest tucked away less than twenty feet off, cradling four beautiful sky blue eggs. Normally, they skulk along the fringes of activity, but the opportunity for sex changes everything for these undemonstrative birds.

One male suddenly flies away, landing atop a tiny spray of growth missed by the hedge trimmer. There, he sings his sharp, sweet, squeaky trill, his tail flickering in a flirty rhythm, always poised to dive back into the safety of cover, when not posing for a female.

Back in February, they were one of the main songsters, but now they remain principally on child and mating duty, the male's singing reduced to short bursts.

♪ **05:56**

The **goldfinches** have finally broken into full chat mode – cheerful little birds with distinctive red faces, unique among Britain's avifauna. They're constant companions in the garden, their bright chatter a year-round soundtrack. When listening for other birds, you often have to tune them out, cutting through their ceaseless twitter. Though the male has a delicate, sweet song, it's rarely heard here. I suspect that's because they're less territorial, content to feed together, perhaps finding safety in numbers. And so, this morning, they add a lively din to the dawn chorus.

This is one of the most familiar birds in our garden. A small flock (charm) made up of mainly youngsters builds and builds by late summer as each subsequent brood joins the fray. Unusually for small birds, they delight in hanging out high up in the tall trees. Even now in early May, the first brood has fledged, and there are three more nests with eggs cradled in the various creepers adorning the house. One is in a honeysuckle on the east side, one in a climbing rose on the south, and one in a climbing hydrangea on the west, right below our bedroom window.

They love teasing out the teasel seeds with their small, pointed beaks all winter, so I leave them to help the goldfinches feed through to April, by which time the first coltsfoot and dandelion seeds are available. Gardens and orchards are their favourite place to nest, not too high up, not too low, often in a small fork in hazel coppice or the faded blooms of lilac. The nest is a neat cup smaller than your hand, like that of a chaffinch, with moss and lichen, and meticulously lined with horsehair and feathers. Four white eggs are usually laid; each is spotted irregularly with various shades of grey and brown.

They, along with the greenfinches, are often found feeding in my vegetable patch, where they are very welcome, as they help reduce the weed seed bank. Historically, they were birds of arable weeds, which are now greatly diminished, and so they find a good living in the kitchen garden.

♪ 05:57

We've heard the occasional short *coo* from **woodpigeons** this morning, but only now does its full-throated summer song ring out. How loud they *coo* – yet in flight, they're oddly silent, save for the sudden clap of wings as they clatter away and the whistle of their wing pinions. They don't join the raucous chorus of jackdaws, rooks, and starlings, whose constant babble of warnings, threats, and scoldings seems to shake the air. When fleeing danger overhead or braving a whistling winter gale, their sheer heft seems to punch them through the sky. But on the lawn, woodpigeons bumble about awkwardly, without grace, scanning aimlessly for clover and chickweed. And if I want to give them some anthropomorphic qualities, they do look pretty gormless.

♪ **06:23**

A very precise, loud songster breaks cover, one of only a handful of birds who sing their names – the **chiffchaff**. He has been singing since he arrived on 22 March, the first of our summer migrants.

His yellow and green plumage is virtually identical to the willow warbler, as he feeds among the like-coloured early leaves. You may distinguish them by their black legs, distinct from the willow warbler's light brown legs. However, their constant movement from branch to stem and stem to leaf means identifying the colour of their legs is somewhat challenging, so look for the persistent flicking of the chiffchaff's tail. Their songs are eons apart, but we do not hear the sweet willow warbler around here, whose song for me is a memory of early spring fishing on the River Usk and the Yorkshire Dales.

As the chiffchaff sang midway up in a lime tree on 23 April, I found his nest, similar to how I found the greenfinch nest. It was the mate bringing back a pigeon feather that caught my eye. She lined her little dome in some dead grass at the foot of a yew hedge, where the cleavers wind their way towards the sun. This is the same quiet corner where the blackcaps nest, and sure enough, my fears were founded when the more aggressive and larger singing blackcap seemed to push the chiffchaff to the other side of the garden. After a week, the nest was abandoned, and I never found another nest.

♪ 06:26

The first **house martin** poked his head out of his nest at 06:26 and chattered briefly before doing a quick loop around the garden over the still frost-crisp lawn and decided it was too early to waste energy and retreated out of sight.

Together with spotted flycatchers, it is the house martins whose return I most eagerly await each spring – that chatter, an ambient soundscape, a babble of human-like dialect, outside my office window. A happiness, I can only liken it to the schoolchildren's playground hubbub. You are not directly involved, but you know it's there, and it reassures you that the world is OK. And then every time a bird leaves the nest, it tweets a double *'spritz, spritz'* as if to say, 'see you later.'

Distinct from the swallow, with their prominent white rump and stumpier tail, house martins are best known for their round nests, made of hundreds of individually collected pellets of mud, under the eaves and porches of our houses.

The first bird – I presume a male – arrived early this year on April 5 to claim one of the nest boxes installed on the east-facing side of our house. A large gable provides a nice drop for the birds as they launch their wings from the nest. I put up four nest boxes last year, because for two successive years running, great spotted woodpeckers hammered away at the poor martins' nest to prey on their chicks. No more Mr Nice Guy with peanuts for you in the winter, you black and white, red-dashed beauties.

This solitary house martin called and called from the box's entrance, followed by little mad dashes into the sky, saying, 'Look at me, I have a lovely home, and I am super fit.' The weather turned distinctly cooler with sharp night frosts, and he took off for a while, so common for house martins in early spring. Where do they go to find a more reliable food source when it's cold? Chew Valley, perhaps, or even all the way back south to France?

Then, on 16 April, his chattering paid off, as a female appeared and accepted his invitation. Both these dates are early for house martins around here, but as always, nature evens things out, and it was not until 19 May that I found the first broken eggshell lying on the ground, roughly split in half, showing a successful hatch.

♪ 06:27

A drake **mallard** does a quick flyby with a solitary quack – probably signalling to his mate somewhere on her nest that it's time for a wash up and feed for breakfast. This pair often comes to my pond in the morning, where she gulps down bills-full of duckweed and oval-leaved pond weed, followed by a good bath. They then loaf around together for around half an hour before she puts in another stint on the nest.

♪ 06:35

Out flies the **pied wagtail** from her nest in the honeysuckle on the house '*chiz-sic, chiz-sic*'. We are all familiar with their bobbing, awkward walk when they hunt for insects on our lawns. I suppose you could call it jaunty, as if their hip joints are playing them up. Or maybe it's the grass tickling them, because it must be hard work for such a small bird. Similar to the house martin, the wagtails like our presence and also have a chatty, friendly sound.

♪ **06:40**

The **coal tit,** although about the same size as a blue tit, seems to be the lesser cousin – always on the edge, far less common. It seems a bit late for the first showing of the day, but maybe the frost means she must brood her youngsters longer to keep them warm, in their nest deep inside a disused water pump in the kitchen garden.

They more than make up for their subtle colours with a louder, more raucous *'cher-tee cher-tee'* compared to blue tits, where they scold you from the hedge line. Now, this may be a member of the titmouse family you're less familiar with. Still, it's easily recognised by the distinctive white stripe running vertically across the nape of its charcoal-coloured head.

Unlike the more numerous blue tits, great tits and long-tailed tits, you will rarely see more than two coal tits at once on your bird feeder, but it does have a unique sound, which I was glad to hear today.

♪ 06:44

You cannot really say **long-tailed tits** sing, and this is partly because they are always together, emitting a continuous communication *'tsee tsee tsee'*.

This year, we had two nests. Unfortunately, on 2 April, I found a dead adult on the lawn. I suspect this was a bird from the nest in the gorse I had planted, as there was no sign of any adults there. The remaining nest, tight in a blackthorn bush, is hard to see, and it was not until 23 April that I saw not two but *three* adults taking food to the young. This 'allofeeding' behaviour, in which young are fed by birds other than the direct parents, is unusual with British birds, and I like to think the parents were getting help from the bird that lost its mate.

On 2 May, parents were still feeding their young in the nest. This is now the danger stage. The chicks are becoming loud and large for the nest, attracting the attention of predators. At least the blackthorn is entirely cloaked in green and a little more hidden. An adult leaves the nest and at once flits after flying insects around the lime trees.

♪ 06:55

A distant single caw from a carrion crow tells the world to keep an eye out, because the black slayer of the small and weak is awake and no doubt hungry.

♪ 07:00

Simultaneously in perfect unison, arms shooting skyward – an instinctive reaction – I shouted *'Hobby!'* just as my photographer friend David shouted *'Cuckoo!'*

A bird had flashed through the garden at head height – gone in a blink. About the size of a mistle thrush, maybe a touch bigger, but smaller than a pigeon, with pointed wings. Too quick for colours, though I caught a darker (but not too dark) back and a lighter (but not too light) front.

Funny how the brain can catch you out. I've never seen or heard a cuckoo in the garden. Still, we do get hobbies in summer – similar size, similar flight line, fast, and direct with pointy wings – familiarity bias, and we have cognitive deficit. There were only two real possibilities, and my brain, dipping into its cache memory, leaned on a sense of 'place' for the answer.

It filtered out the low height of the flight, the complete absence of rapid wing beat, the darkness of the head, which, at that distance, should have been apparent, and the lack of any warning from the garden's usual sentinels. The passerines, especially the house martins, always raise the alarm when a hobby is near.

We conferred, umpires on the green, and taking all in all, we settled for cuckoo. It was the spitting image of the cuckoo flying through an orchard in one of the old Ladybird books – *What to Look for in Spring*. Now that image is to the fore of my brain, a bird slightly breast-side on wings back, probably in full migration mode, traveling fast northeast.

What's more remarkable is that we were there to see it. I haven't seen a cuckoo from the garden since I was about ten years old. I remember the moment clearly – I was burying a young sparrow I'd tried to keep alive after it fell from the nest. The yin and yang of it has remained with me all my life; the sadness of one bird's death, and the delight of witnessing another – a cuckoo I'd often heard but never seen.

When I was a child, we once had a cuckoo chick raised by a pair of dunnocks, but of course, you never see the female. She's there for a second, slipping in to lay her egg – and then gone, as if she were never there.

 *It was not until 21 May that I saw my first hobby of the year fly through the garden – an amazing, swift, direct flight powered*

by swept-back scythe-like wings. There was no meandering laziness, just absolute intent to disturb something, catch a juvenile bird off guard, and chase it to the ground.

It was on precisely the same flightline as the cuckoo two weeks earlier, although higher in the sky, flying in a gap between the back of the house and the tall larch and beech trees.

If you were to describe a cuckoo, you'd probably place it somewhere between a female sparrowhawk and a hobby. It shares the sparrowhawk's size, long tail, and similar colouring, but its flight is more like the hobby's – direct and swift, with pointed wings rather than the hawk's broader, rounded ones. Before science introduced us to migration, some people thought cuckoos turned into hawks in winter!

♪ 07:01

The local pair of **red kites** seems to have decided it's finally warm enough to warrant their first lazy sortie of the morning. Long, slow flaps as they gather altitude before hanging in the air. Old-fashioned drones, each with a pair of eyes scanning below for anything worth investigating. They may not be agile like a hawk, and true, their legs are a little weaker than a buzzard's, but don't let anyone tell you they are just scavengers. Their graceful, often wheeling flight, steered by their forked tail silhouetted clearly in the sky, belies the peril their shadow paints on any ground-nesting bird below. Even their song hides their menace. A gentle, subservient '*whew, heh, heh, heh*'. Never judge a book by its cover.

They are our second most common bird of prey, sandwiched between the buzzard first, the tawny owl third, and the sparrowhawk fourth. Their acrobatic flight has been described as aerial ballet, but it is very grounded, rooted to what is happening on the earth below. A reaction to something foody in their vision, sending a pulsating vibe to that all-important tiller – the red-ochre forked tail.

In a watery world, a pike spins on quivering pectoral fins,
its tail driving the thrust.
In the sky, the kite wheels on its tail –
A twist, a dip, a forked fulcrum positioning the wings
before powering, their fixed gaze down to the unfortunate.

♪ 07:15

Here's a bird you'd think could never hide, with colours as showy as any in the UK. The **bullfinch** – at least the male – is unmistakable: bright red underparts, a striking black cap, and a soft grey back. And yet, often, you'll notice it only as it slips away, that flash of a white rump – like a fleeting house martin – and its simple, repetitive, plaintive call: '*deu… deu…*' That's what gave it away this morning, coming from the top of a beech hedge. Always together as a pair, they maintain constant contact through a shared noise, leading their own lives, never in the company of others.

I never found their nest this year, but they were successful, with a family flying around the garden late June and early July, again with that unmistakable 'deu, deu' and flash of the white rump. Last year, they nested quite late, in August, tucked deep inside an impenetrable stretch of hawthorn hedge. I only found them by chance, their chunky-billed chicks like miniature versions of the adults. They're often among the last of the songbirds to nest, which is something to bear in mind when planning hedge cutting. Like the greenfinch, they nest close to the side and top of the hedge, especially in an evergreen (yew or holly) growing through, say, beech or privet. Good marketing for mixed hedges!

♪ 07:43

On the very top branch of our big larch tree, a **starling** is now singing – his nest next door in a hole under the eaves. They are rarely seen or heard here in the village until November, when large flocks, probably from the Continent, gather to feed among the sheep.

My childhood was filled with their songs as a pair always nested under a loose tile, but today, it is the unfamiliarity of the call that catches my ear. This large larch tree in the centre of the garden is a magnet for many passing birds, especially the larger beasties, such as red kites and buzzards, a convenient command post, or, as today, the perfect soap box to sell your wares.

House sparrows were the sound of my youth, and so too were starlings. This proud bird with his merry jig of a song – a jumble of primary school playground chatter, chuckles, and mechanical clicks mysteriously descending into soft croons before a startlingly long whistle: an ornithological Tower of Babel. Just a dot in the sky, his coat of many metallic colours, each feather tipped in white, is lost in the glare of the horizon.

Starlings are more numerous around here in the winter, with large flocks building up by February before they disperse back to their breeding territories. As the day darkens in January, swift-flying flocks of between twenty and a few hundred birds fly across the garden to the southwest. Always in this direction –

the sound of their wings makes you look up into the sky. Exactly where they congregate and perform their murmuration before roosting, I have no idea. I once tried to follow them in a car, but I lost them somewhere crossing Tan Hill and down into the Pewsey Vale.

Back to the large larch tree – I assume it was planted around the time the house was built. I'd estimate its age at around 150 years. That would make sense, as the Victorians had a great admiration for pine trees, particularly larches, due in part to their fondness for Scotland, where these trees were widely planted as fast-growing timber for pit props, fencing, boats, and telegraph poles. Bringing a sense of the Scottish landscape, a 'place' to Wiltshire would have appealed to the Victorian taste for estate planning, which blended utility with aesthetic appeal. Adding to its charm is the fact that larch is the only deciduous conifer – its soft, feathery, green needles now at their finest, each tuft bursting from knobby beads all along the twigs. Nestled among these needles are the beautiful purple female flowers, which Tennyson described as 'rosey plumlets', another reason I think of it as a 'Victorian tree'.

In northern plantations of conifers, the larch stands out among the ranks of dark pines in its happy spring verdancy, and again in the autumn, where it turns the hillsides yellow. Here in the garden, it contrasts with the copper beech.

It is, however, one of only three remaining from an original five, judging by two weathered stumps in the garden, and although in its prime, it is vulnerable to wind damage and bough break when the branches are laden with cones.

I've already mentioned how mistle thrushes favour it as a nesting tree, but it's also much loved by goldfinches – see the photograph of their nest on the back cover. The neatly woven nest is lost from sight, where its lichen weavings hide among the lichen-encrusted branches. Looking inside the cup, each egg is protected on a soft bed of horsehair, spider web, and sheep wool.

♪ **07:46**

I had checked the barn next door an hour earlier to see the **swallows** still sitting tight on a rafter by their nest, waiting for the earth to warm up. Finally, at 07:46, the first of the pair came twinkling over the garden and across to the fields beyond. I know many people are confused about distinguishing between swallows and house martins, but a key differentiator is their flight pattern. A swallow is masterful, effortless, and languid all at once, a floating flight unlike the still masterful but jerky short strokes of the house martin. 'Breaststroke' versus the 'crawl'.

The swallow's song is a series of *'whet'*, either as a solitary, sometimes harsh note, or, as this morning, a more melodious series of rapid *'whet whet'* so sweet it seems it has not a harsh word to say to anybody. When first arriving in spring, their song is more energetic, and bubbling, while later, as migration draws near in September, it is at its most lovely, matching the melancholy of the robin.

This pair has made their nest at the apex of the barn rafters, in the typical highest, darkest vantage point they can find, a strategy that complements their association with humans.

 *On 20 May, amidst the loose flotsam of misplaced feathers, globs of mud and other detritus left over from building their nest, were clean, broken, white eggshells. Here was the reward for the long migration here from South Africa – the proof their young had hatched, safeguarding the species, building resilience, at least for another year.*

♪ 11:00

On the southeast corner of our house, tucked beneath the eaves, is a swallow nest box – never claimed by swallows, but faithfully used by **spotted flycatchers** for the past six years. A flicker of movement catches my eye as one of these understated little birds flits from the shadows beneath the eaves to perch on the guttering, as if it had never left since last summer. They are back – God bless them.

They went on to successfully fledge a brood of four youngsters, and by early July had a second nest, this time in the open bay barn, perched directly atop a real swallow nest. There's clearly some kind of symbiosis at play between these birds, swallows, and us humans, the guardian angels.

♪ 11:01

As if on cue, and not to be outdone, several **house martins** begin nest prospecting on the east side of the house, no doubt drawn in by the noise and sight of the established pair. And of course, they fight, tussling each other to the ground. Why? When there are three identical empty boxes ten feet to their right.

Nature, and I include humans here, always thinks someone else has something better. The grass is always greener on the other side. Like fishing with a worm dangling amongst a shoal, nothing stirs, until you twitch the rod to pull away the bait, one fish turns to move, then everyone pounces. Being left out would be tragic.

 *A week later, the madness stops, and a pair takes over one of the empty boxes. By the beginning of June, the first brood is almost ready to fly – phew! Building their own nests takes time and is challenging, especially in a dry spring. My hope is the new boxes will allow the martins to have more time to raise multiple broods in a single season.*

Everything in the garden quietens down – almost a hush.

PART
TWO

Coal tit

MIDDAY
Siesta

♪ **12:30**

For the most part, the birds have sunk quietly into themselves, save for the soft *'seep seep'* of young blackbirds and the constant cries of hungry blue tit chicks calling from a nest box. A blackcap bathes in the bird bath, dipping its head as it pushes water over its back. These 'wash stations,' once a staple of gardens, seem to have fallen from fashion, yet they are eagerly sought in hot weather, especially when birds are nest-bound for long stretches of incubation. I often watch great tits, blue tits and robins splash through a quick rinse, but it is the blackcap that lingers longest. Perhaps the water draws them to the garden, or perhaps it is the safety halo of its proximity to the house.

Fast forward a couple of months to early August, and the dawn chorus was a very different affair. Most of the small passerines were now moulting their primary feathers, skulking quietly so as not to draw attention to themselves, away from prying eyes. Gone were the melodies, and 5am saw me woken by harsher notes, not music, not background sounds, but big noise.

The grating, jarring, piercing, and yes, really whining screech of the 'spoilt' buzzard fledgling stirs me rudely.

'Kee-ah, kee-ah, kee-ah' and on and on it goes. This is not the gentle, sometimes soporific 'mewing' of an adult buzzard.

The poor parents are nowhere near the nest, but sat hunched three hundred yards away from this plaintive begging, a demand for food. I am not so lucky. I'm much nearer and the noise is awful.

To make absolutely sure that I will not drop back to sleep, a green woodpecker rocks up on the larch tree with its wild echoing laugh, the 'yaffle'. He jubilantly mocks the buzzard with a wild, echoing laugh, something like a hurried 'klu, klu, klu, klu' spat out from the trees.

It's like a witch cackling in the garden, a woodland spirit. In folklore, the green woodpecker was said to have betrayed a secret and was cursed forevermore to hammer on trees, laughing at its own fate. It appears to be laughing at me for still being in bed, but it will vanish as soon as I poke my head out of the window – that will be the 'spirit' bit.

And then the woodpigeons do that weird, clapping courtship stuff when they bang their wings together, a noise too sudden to ignore, as if someone is hitting you in the face with a large soft glove.

Now I am truly awake. Not the gentle alarm of May, but the full-on reminder of Nature's disinclination to bend to our powers.

Later in the same day, in August, early evening, I find myself in the stillness of a pine wood. Again, the dawn chorus of May is a past relic of the year, faded along with the fresh green growth, as I step through the dry and brittle understorey, the blackberry shoots twisted pale as they try to prevent moisture loss. An occasional tree catches the falling sunlight – no birdsong except for another young buzzard. I disturb a young roe deer, who appears ghost-like from nowhere.

A young buck catches her scent, his guttural bark an abrupt and amorous cough hard to pin down among the trees – another spirit of the woods, and a reminder we are now in August.

How to attract birds to a garden

This is a good time to explore in more detail how, by midday, a garden can produce over 30 species of birds in just over six hours, and even more telling, up to 20 species nesting.

A varied mix of managed plant species – across different ages and heights – supports
• abundant insect life (food)
• diverse habitat (shelter)
• and minimal disturbance (predators)

All sustained by chemical-free practices that nurture healthy soils and fungal networks.

Essentially, I am managing my garden like a wood, but maximising diversity of species and the 'open bits'.

Left entirely to rewild, diversity would decline over time as dominant species take hold. Although still preferable to intensive farming, unmanaged land can lack the richness that careful, informed stewardship can provide. For millennia, humans have helped shape diverse ecosystems – but in our pursuit of efficiency, combined with the input of chemicals and increased disturbance, we've begun to unravel the very balance we once helped build.

Through thoughtful gardening, we can recreate diverse habitats without extra work, if we can give ourselves a good talking-to about our obsession and craziness with tidiness. Most of our so-called 'garden birds' are actually woodland birds, making the most of the opportunities we nurture for them.

The word 'glade' comes to mind, which in Old English meant a 'clearing in the wood', related to the Old German and Norse words 'klad' and 'kladre'. This is what you are trying to recreate – a mix of shade and light.

A recent report by the Woodland Trust ('State of the UK's woods and Trees') discusses how, although we marginally increased our tree cover in the UK from 13.2% in 2020 to 13.4% in 2024, we have seen a reduction in *diversity* in terms of different ages, conditions, and sizes.

The report by Abigail Bunker, director of conservation for the Woodland Trust, discusses two aspects of woodland improvement, structure and composition, which can also apply to your garden.

She highlights the significant decline in the richness and complexity of biodiversity in our woodlands, particularly the loss of older trees and the disappearance of open glades that allow younger trees to establish. One striking statistic she cites is that 46% of woods contain no deadwood at all, which is pretty bad when you consider that around a quarter of all species depend on deadwood at some stage of their life cycle.

Read that again and think about how you can mitigate some of these challenges within your own garden.

When you fell a tree, it does not have to be cut right down to the ground. Not all the logs or brush have to be cleared away.

Build your garden bottom upwards from the soil to fungi, to plants, to insects and invertebrates, and the birds and the wildlife will follow.

Here, I draw out the key elements of the woodland report and highlight those particularly relevant to our gardens and the wildlife they support.

Structure

Not every weed is your enemy, and a locally adapted mix of plants will naturally support a locally adapted mix of birds. Abigail describes this process of natural regeneration as vital for the future of our woodlands because it builds resilience to climate change by increasing genetic diversity, helping trees adapt to local conditions. Trees that establish themselves in this way often prove more robust than those that are planted, in the same way that weeds flourish so successfully. In addition, naturally regenerated landscapes tend to be richer and more beneficial for wildlife.

 **Understanding what grows well in your garden is halfway to understanding what wildlife it will attract.**

Deadwood

A vegetable gardener I know in the Tropics once spent two hours explaining to me the importance of deadwood and how it can boost soil health by encouraging fungi and welcoming natural pest predators like beetles, many of which need decaying wood during their larval stage. Since then, I've surrounded my vegetable beds with logs. I've also left two large dead trees to decay slowly and safely where they stand, rather than felling them. And I've added a few log piles here and there – little ecosystems in their own right – all helping to bring the soil to life.

Abigail refers to dead wood as decaying wood, since it is very much alive, with an estimated 500 arthropod individuals living in each litre of wood from dead branches, and an average of 2,500 arthropods inhabiting each kilogram of 'wood mould'. This decaying wood is useful whether standing as part of a tree, hollow, or lying on the woodland floor. Savernake Forest, near where I live, is famous for its 33 ancient oak trees, many of which are hollow, with some even fallen over. This all adds to the forest's biodiversity, since decaying wood plays a disproportionate role in a thriving ecosystem. The UK Woodland Assurance Standard (UKWAS) includes recommendations for deadwood management as part of its certification standards for sustainable woodland.

 **Leaving deadwood in the garden is part of its managed maintenance.**

Vertical structure

Since an estimated 30% of forest-dwelling birds use tree cavities, variation in the different heights of a woodland is essential, and it is well known that the lack of availability of a range of different types of cavities is a limitation for bird populations. Diseases and windblow vary with a tree's age, and, in turn, these various structures not only increase the surface area of your garden, your sanctuary, but also provide different habitats for feeding, nesting, shelter, and roosting.

There was a shift toward fewer, larger trees from 1971 to 2022 across surveyed woodlands, with a corresponding reduction in trees of different ages, but an increase in understorey holly, probably due to a warming climate. Add to this greater pressure from deer grazing, and our woods become less attractive to many species, hence the importance of our gardens.

Remember, it's not just the obvious holes in a tree, but the less obvious crinkles and cavities in the bark, and all the lichens and mosses which provide additional homes for insects, especially their dormant eggs, over winter. And the birds need all this.

Composition

The make-up of a woodland affects how well it can cope with change. Woodlands with greater species and age diversity are generally more resilient. Different species overlap in the roles in the ecosystem. For example, one species may help fix nitrogen, another pollinates plants, another breaks down dead material. If one species declines, another can often continue that role.

For this reason, many measures of woodland health focus on species diversity, including ground flora and the number of native trees.

Diversity equals greater resilience, which is important with current challenges such as climate change. Make your garden more resilient.

Nativeness

Native species have evolved alongside other native plants and animals, which helps support greater biodiversity. For example, in the UK, around 2,300 species – including birds, fungi, insects, and mammals – are associated with oak trees such as Sessile Oak and

English Oak. Of these, 326 species depend entirely on oak, and it would take many other tree species combined to support the same range of wildlife.

 **Why would you plant a foreign non-fruit-bearing plant in your garden?**

Open spaces
Around 50% of native woods in Britain have less than 10% open space (glades), a figure that has declined significantly between 1971 and 2021, placing many woodlands in an unfavourable condition.

 **This is where gardens can play a role. Nature thrives on edges, where habitats meet. Even a small garden can create these conditions by allowing for woodland edges or small glades that bring light and variety, helping to support more wildlife.**

♪ **12:45**
With the birds seemingly at rest, sound is limited to the bees. Today we have **Early bumble bees, Buff-tailed bumble bees, Hairy-footed Flower Bees**, and **White-tailed bumble bees**. As May moves into summer, we will be joined by the big **Orange-tailed bumble bees**.

I encourage bumble bees into the garden with early pulmonaria, wild violets, pussy willow, and white dead-nettle – crucial food sources before the abundance of summer blooms fills the lands. This early nourishment is often overlooked, but when planted in a sheltered, east-facing spot to catch the morning sun, it allows a wide range of insects to begin foraging sooner in the warmth. The white dead-nettles are still growing strong, and the comfrey now just coming into its own is alive with particularly carder bees and white-tailed bumbles.

The dry weather is beginning to take its toll on the butterflies. A **small white** stretches out its long proboscis, drawing moisture from the damp soil where I watered the beetroot and carrot seedlings last night. Perhaps it's also seeking out trace minerals – but it's butterfly behaviour I've noticed often this year, not just in small whites but also in brimstones, peacocks, and red admirals.

In full bloom today is the hawthorn. This morning it shone through in the dawn picture, matching the frosty grass with its snowy boughs.

Overlooked for most of the season, its common name, 'May', is very apt, attaining peak perfection now – a bloom for 'Chelsea'. It is bejewelled, its roots still drawing water from deep below. Though always a small tree – more a bush on a trunk – we have a particularly tall specimen, its grizzled bark twisted like an old rope.

Today, it takes centre stage, having bloomed after the earlier flushes of blackthorn, followed by cherry and the wild crab apples, before it too will yield place to the frothy plates of elderflower in June.

♪ 13:00

The **coal tits** I mentioned earlier often attempt to nest in a disused cast-iron hand pump in the kitchen garden. I'm never quite sure whether they succeed – or perhaps I'm not around to see. This has been going on for ten years, which raises the question: how do they know it's there? They cannot possibly be the original pair. And why do coal tits favour it, while their close cousins, the blue tits, show no interest at all?

If you imagine a water pump, the spout comes out perpendicular to the wall, and then curves downwards to the ground, so to enter, the birds are forced to fly up inside it vertically, and to exit they have to drop vertically to leave – quite a feat. Additionally, it is attached to a south-facing wall, exposed to direct sunlight. This must be a warm, cosy, and predator-proof home at night, but it warms up considerably during the day.

These birds are used to human presence, so we set up the camera four metres away to try to capture this aerial dexterity. Between 13:00 and 15:00, poor David stands then sits patiently with a camera, trying to catch the exact moment the birds appear. The birds are returning only every 30 minutes, with relatively long brood periods in between. As a professional wildlife cameraman, David remains undaunted, and I keep him well-stocked with food and beverages, but capturing the exact millisecond a bird flies in or out is proving difficult.

Attached to the same wall as the pump is an espaliered pear tree. In the blink of an eye, the parents come over the wall, flying through a small gap in the pear leaves, straight to the pump entrance. Finger on the camera shutter or not, there is no time to react. As for catching them leaving the nest, that is like playing whack-a-mole.

We devise a plan – I will spot one of the parents before they reach the wall, and at the exact moment they fly, I will say '*now*'. This gives David enough time to react and press the button (*see photo back cover*). Knowing the bird is in the nest makes it a little easier to anticipate its exit. Two fantastic shots are taken in and out in mid-flight. What you notice now is that the bird drops out of the tap, wings folded, and conversely, on the return, at the last minute, folds them again to fit inside the pump.

 *A week later, the parents have stepped up foraging, and are feeding the chicks every three minutes – trying to spot the young leaving will be my next challenge. Well, I did miss it, but it was sometime on Monday, 26 May.*

House Martins

AFTERNOON TEA

At 15:00, the sun creeps out. Instantaneously, the garden is back in full swing – goldfinch, house martin, woodpigeon, wren and robin all singing together, while the bumble bees adorn the comfrey. Now this is a plant everyone should grow for the bees alone, if not for the natural potassium-rich tomato feed you can make from its leaves. As the delicately mauve and pink tubular flowers open, they droop towards the ground, compelling bumble bees to hang upside down, burying their heads as they seek the nectar in the base of the bloom, their weight setting off a ripple, trembling through each flower cluster.

♪ **15:10**

Like a small boy whistling a single repetitive note, content with a candy bar, but so much louder than any sound we can make, a **nuthatch** passes through the garden. It's an unmistakable, urgent sound, usually coming from relatively high up in a tree – *'tui, tui, tui'*. Unlike the treecreeper, which always climbs up tree trunks and branches from the bottom up, the nuthatch can be found upwards, sideways, or downwards.

Last year, the nuthatches nested in a disused great spotted woodpecker hole in our sugar maple, making quite a racket throughout April before quietening down to incubate their eggs and feed their young. Typically, nuthatches in the UK reduce the size of the entrance hole to their nests with mud and clay to form a safer nest chamber. Then they line these nests with dried leaves, and particularly Scots pine bark scales. This prompts one of those natural history questions – is that why they nested here? Because of the proximity of the Scots pine trees?

On 30 May, three nuthatch fledglings crash-landed into the kitchen garden – their noisy arrival instantly recognisable. Like many boisterous youngsters, it felt as though the whole garden was alive with nuthatches, when in fact there were only these three.

♪ 15:30

The sun has called up a slight breeze, and the flycatcher now flies lower to the ground, sometimes even landing among the grass. Subject to weather conditions, they hold individual perches, like fishing posts, to fly down passing insects. When it's windy, they hunt from the hazel trees sheltering a small lawn to the west of the house. When it is raining, they seek the lower boughs protected by the trees, and yet when the sky is clear and the air is still, they seek the very top of the roof where some invisible boundary separates the owners of a nest on the east of the house, and the owners of the nest on the west of the house.

In ten years, I have never seen either stray off their patch. Creatures of habit, they are site-faithful each year, and I am now beholden to look after them. Like it or not, they are my responsibility. The thought ages me. Who will maintain and manage the garden to help them when I am gone? I will leave a covenant on the house, stipulating that any new owners must read this book. Please, dear reader, pass on this book to mitigate land development and disconnection from nature.

Meanwhile, the goldfinches, which typically feed on seeds on the ground, use the high branches for social companionship. This 'place' identity helps you identify each bird species. If your eyes fail or your auditory recognition is poor, 'place' gives you the edge.

This is all part of 'jizz', a term first used by Thomas Coward in his *Country Diary* column for the *Manchester Guardian* of 6 December 1921. He, in turn, attributed it to 'a west-coast Irishman' and explained:

'If we are walking on the road and see, far ahead, someone whom we recognise although we can neither distinguish features nor particular clothes, we may be certain that we are not mistaken; there is something in the carriage, the walk, the general appearance which is familiar; it is, in fact, the individual's jizz.'

There are several theories as to the etymology of 'jizz':

• From the military term 'GIS' (general impression and shape).
• Possible contraction of 'just is' (in the sense that a particular bird species 'just is' that species).

Knowledge gleamed through both physical and behavioural characteristics, as well as place, over many years of experience. It covers all the reasons why I know which bird is which, and to explain it will make my brain hurt, and still perhaps you will not get it. It is a wealth of accumulated knowledge, so that individual characteristics, by which everyone learns, go out of the window. That bird, that butterfly, they are what they are and individual characteristics are just there for our confirmation. It is an art form every bit as skilled as the artist who captures the 'jizz' in a portrait.

I just know.

♪ **15:40**

A **kestrel** flies above, arcing abruptly to the south, no doubt unsure of our presence. They are relatively common along the valley, but more noticeable this time of year in the garden when they have extra mouths to feed. They beat the air for food; like a dream I am flyfishing, casting into the clouds in vain, in hope… We can only dream of the kestrel's eyes, holding steady on the wing as they scan the world, natural killer drones. In the past, I saw more kestrels, and I do wonder if the increase in buzzards, crows and red kites has pushed them out. No scientific evidence, just an anecdotal observation.

What I do know for sure is that our garden hosts a high density of **field voles**. From above, the kestrel's remarkable ability to see ultraviolet (UV) traces – urine trails invisible to us – marks the garden as a rich vole territory worth investigating. Worth dropping in height for closer inspection, worth burning wing muscles to hold that steady gaze on coloured prisms below, glimpses of a world we are only now discovering through AI and the use of drones.

Glimpsing with our naked eye connects our brain to experience and feeling. Technology will morph these glimpses into hard data points and remote surveys, and this tech monitoring will be stripped of all the intimacy and wonder that direct perception brings.

♪ 16:03

Somewhere high up in the lime trees, there is a barely perceptible *'Chwit-chwit'* – a high-pitched trill. It's a **treecreeper**, that wonderful delight of a bird.

It's camouflaged like a trout swimming erratically up tree trunks with brown streaks above and white underparts, although at first glance, you think you are seeing a mouse. They're never still, and I'm sure they're far more common than their occasional sightings suggest.

On 2 June, I found the whole treecreeper family attached to some birch trees waiting to be fed. This is not your typical group of youngsters sitting in a line – they are all spaced out at individual angles, pointing skywards, hidden among the gnarly birch bark. To find the adults, keep a close eye on the bottom of the tree, since they constantly repeat their hunt from the bottom upwards, and then fly down again. They will allow you to observe from a few feet away as they busy themselves in a relentless search for food.

♪ 16:08

In the wildflower blocks of my garden, the red campion is approaching 'peak pink'. I introduced this flower to the garden to enrich the flower palette between the fading bluebells and the towering foxgloves. Called red campion, the petals display a complex spectrum of pinks – some deep magenta, others a lighter rose, the same hue of the dog rose in the hedge. As each bloom ages, it traces the full range of tints, fading from the original opening bright cerise to that of a dead geranium petal in the greenhouse. Even more important, its beauty attracts insects, and here it draws in a feeding **brimstone**.

This 'utterly butterly' yellow butterfly flies drunkenly across the garden from side to side. It looks like it is careering into the hedge for stability, before launching off in another direction at the last moment to take a different tack, before alighting on the freshest magenta bloom it can find – such contrast to the swift-flying

painted lady, which briefly darts across the garden a little later.

To watch a butterfly in flight is one thing, but often more captivating are the intricate patterns – the hieroglyphics etched on the underside of the wings, especially the hind wings. We all recognise the beautiful male orange tip with his freshly emerged bright tangerine wing tips, which after a few days fade, just like the red campion flowers, to a softer apricot, but how many of us have studied the drab colourless female?

Without the male's distinctive orange tips, she is often mistaken for a small white, the ordinary cabbage white. But look more closely at her underwings, and you'll find a delicate green marbling set against a white background. Like the feathers of some birds, a butterfly's colours can deceive the eye. That soft green isn't pigment at all, but a mosaic of bright yellow and black scales, arranged in a way that resembles a patterned green lichen or moss on a weathered stone.

I always try to leave lady's smock (cuckoo flowers) growing in the garden since it is a favoured food plant for their caterpillars, and the same goes for sweet rocket.

Today we have seen **peacock**, painted lady, **orange tip**, brimstone, and **holly blue** – but soon we will be joined by the first speckled wood and green-veined white of the year.

♪ 16:12

A **lesser black back gull** flies high, leisurely, with that glide and flap flight, southeast – no doubt heading towards one of the roof nests on the trading estate in Devizes. Their primary feeding place, this time of year, is the refuse dump just west of Wootton Bassett, while a little earlier in the year, I watched them from across the river clearing up the afterbirth from the newly born lambs. This sea bird enjoying life so far from the sea has nothing to do with me, but watching their flight, their long, peloton arrows cross the evening sky, is relaxing.

♪ 16:37

Two mallard drakes fly quickly across the garden chasing a female, with one low, long, drawn-out *'quaaaaak!'* and they are gone.

The female mallard nests next door but takes a break from incubation each afternoon, flying over for a quick wash and feed in our pond before snoozing on the lawn. Now, ducks being ducks, her mate – the drake – always tags along. It's a thoughtful gesture on the surface, but it has more to do with jealousy and maintaining a competitive edge. I suspect it was him just now, defending his mate from an overzealous-intruder.

♪ **16:48**

A **crow** lets out his whingeing, haggling cry – a clear announcement of what's unfolding. It's the constant game of cat and mouse: a pair of carrion crows has a nest in a tall lime tree across the meadow by the river, and they don't take kindly to visitors.

Whenever a **red kite** flaps lazily toward the tree, the crows explode into action, cawing furiously, beaks open and poised to strike. They mean business, running down the intruder with relentless aggression, chasing it right over our garden, and another four hundred yards, well out of harm's way.

An unguarded crow's nest is easy pickings for a kite, which responds with a mewing, defensive whine, twisting through the air in tumbling attempts to shake off the black irritant. Calm returns – but only until the next time.

Peace is short-lived. The **mistle thrush** has seen a threat and '*churrs*' its way from the larch tree to the sycamore, ready for battle. What is going on? My garden can shift from serenity to a battleground in an instant. This is not an aerial threat; something is hiding in the leaves. Even Mrs Mistle Thrush leaves her nest to offer encouragement and support. The rest of the garden bird community has fallen silent, frozen in fear, as still as the tree trunks, holding their cover.

This can only mean one thing: **sparrowhawk**. Somewhere among the green foliage, darkening the gloom in a spattered patch of sun, a pair of the brightest yellow eyes flash death, annoyed by the demented, disrupting mistle thrushes. A chaffinch also sounds the alarm with his characteristic '*spink, spink, spink*'.

I like seeing the sparrowhawks, but I fear my garden will become breakfast, lunch, and supper, so I run over, clapping my hands, and sure enough, a sparrowhawk flies out, now visible to all the birds. They are emboldened, and the cohort flies off in hot pursuit, led by the swallows. On the ground below, I find the intended menu – a chaffinch fledgling dressed in the muted colours of the female bird – I pick him up and let him fall into the arms of the sheltering cow parsley and red campion. 'Learn your lesson, little one, and stay out of harm's way until you are fully grown.'

Am I playing God? Yes. I wouldn't have to if everyone gardened with nature in mind. But they don't – and so my garden creation stands alone, an island of safety in a hostile sea. And it's an island I will defend. It all begins with no chemicals (even if I do have blackfly on my broad beans!), and no chemicals helps the fungi and the insects, which in turn bring in the birds. Key is the patchwork of plants, the ground, the low, the medium, and the tall, all of which create diversity. 'Leave it all alone,' some would say, 'rewild it,' but then it would become a battlefield with no General to dictate terms, until ultimately a tree canopy took control.

Earlier in the year, the young growing foxes, with their insatiable appetites, drove parents to be ever more brazen in their search for food, prowling the perimeter of my chicken coop, waking me up at night with their barking cough. By mid-May, the buzzards, kites, carrion crows, sparrowhawks, and magpies also have extra mouths to feed, so they rampage across the garden, ever more rapacious, disturbing the peace. Their want is greatest just before their young fledge, when they are still confined to the nest and they urge their parents forth with gaping mouths and squawks, to scour the hinterland ever more.

Swallows never returned to nest in my barn after a sparrowhawk took their young one by one, three years ago, and the great spotted woodpeckers emptied my house martin nests by drilling holes through the mud ramparts.

The tragedy and wonders of nature are all here, rampant around the house.

Long Tailed Tits

DUSK
Settling in for the evening

♪ **17:00**

Refreshingly, the sun slips behind a cloud – a welcome respite after our early start to the day – and the garden seems to take the hint, settling into a gentler rhythm. For us, it's the perfect cue to pause for a well-earned glass of Pimms. We haven't been singing all day, but it's been intense enough, especially with the temperature fluctuating by a good 22 degrees, and there's the physical tiredness from constantly straining one's ears and scanning the skies.

I can see the fine bristles, pale and translucent, on the red campion stems, backlit by the evening light, as the pink flowers droop under the weight of visiting bumble bees, one by one. A tremor reverberates along their path. Beneath one of the stone slabs that form a path through the wildflower block, these furry *Bombus terrestris* have made their nest, sheltered from weather and hidden from enemies. Their low, steady hum lulls us away from their industrious work, like the slow rhythmic wingbeat of a fast-flying goose compared to the rapid beats of a slower partridge.

Our brains become bewitched, muddled by blending sound with sight.

A **spotted flycatcher** launches itself at a passing insect, ignoring the general haze of smaller midges. It picks out the biggest protein for the least effort – no escape, as an audible snap seals the insect's fate. Above the lawn, house martins turn and chatter, finding sustenance in the thickening dusk, alive with darting midges and drifting lacewings. These evenings, this bounty is what drew them from Africa in the first place. To build up their strength to lay their clutches for future generations.

♪ 18:30

All day, the calls of **long-tailed tits** have filled the air, and I kept checking their nest for any hint of activity, but it remained still and silent. Then, nature revealed its secret.

At 6pm, my attention was caught by what I thought was the sound of young blue tits calling from the holly above our heads. As I took a step closer to investigate, an adult long-tailed tit flitted across from the cherry tree, all the time calling its distinctive *'tsee-tsee-tsee'*.

And then it dawned on me – these aren't blue tit youngsters at all. The fledglings' calls are subtly different from their parents'. Sure enough, there they are: four restless young long-tailed tits, all clamouring to be fed.

Their bright orange gapes glow among the dark holly leaves, each mouth framed by yellow gape flanges at the corners, thrust forward on outstretched necks as they beg for food. Nearly as large as their parents now, they are softer in hue – greyer, like young chaffinches – and their tails remain short and stubby. Success!

A week later, a jay found their old nest and pulled it to pieces, hoping for a meal. The beautiful lichen, moss, and feathers were ensnared in tatters among the blackthorn twigs. Too late this time, my friend!

Magpies dive straight into thickets and hedges to find nests, storming through the centre to find that precious silhouette against the sky, while the jay searches among open trees, bouncing boldly along the branches looking to flush some bird into revealing its nest. This brings him rewards in the garden among the larch trees with goldcrest and goldfinch nests.

♪ 20:00

The honeysuckle wrapped around the north-eastern corner of the house now mingles with the scent of sweet rocket, filling the air, ready for the night time pollinators. The perfume will be over in three weeks, but now it gently ushers in the dark. It reminds me to walk over to the lilac, to bury my face in the mauve blooms and drink in their scent.

♪ 20:05

Two **Canada geese** honk their way east. There is constant movement throughout the year between some ponds at Marlborough College, which were excavated next to the River Kennet, and a seasonal vernal pool located further upstream, to the west, at West Overton. Due to the heavy winter rains, this pool is larger than usual and will remain long enough for geese to raise some goslings before it recedes back to the river, before ultimately soaking into the chalk.

♪ **20:08**

Walking along the beech hedge, a subtle rustling in the dried copper leaves of last year betrays a **rabbit**, which now bolts across the lawn – its white scut a warning to all the other rabbits. Be alert! But there are no other rabbits to warn. If myxomatosis wiped out 98% of their population in the last century, before a specific immunity crossed the generations, they now contend with another existential threat – Rabbit Haemorrhagic Disease (RHD). This widespread virus rapidly destroys liver cells and disrupts blood clotting, causing internal bleeding in the liver, lungs, and other organs. It has devastated our rabbits in Wiltshire and is particularly harsh on the young. This rabbit and his mate have been here about the beech hedge all winter, where they dug a brood chamber, but I have seen no young this year.

I happily tolerate rabbits in the garden, harvesting them occasionally for their organic, fat-free, and wonderfully clean, white meat. Still, the population has now been low for several years, and this pair in the garden is a bonus.

♪ **20:10**

Two chaffinches have just started singing their hearts out. With the evening air cooling faster near the ground, sound carries further, refracted earthward rather than dispersed skyward. Their song, so often drowned in the noise of the day, is now an 'evening carry' with purity and reach.

These two birds are now on a one-way journey to combat, neither can be ignored, and there are no other distractions to intervene. Unable to out-sing each other, they resort to the tactics of the playground, and a fight breaks out. Down they tumble from the paper-leaved maple, a twirling ball of feathers, claws, beaks, and shrieks, a ball which rolls along the grass, before an invisible referee says '*Enough!*' and they fly back to their respective territories. Not another peep all evening.

Chaffinch nests are very similar to that of the goldfinch – best described as 'neat', and often surprisingly exposed, relying on natural camouflage to blend among their surroundings; they are hard to find. Where most birds bury their nests in the deepest tangle of growth, I find the chaffinches' cup on the bare branches of elder and cherry, seemingly inviting danger. But when that danger arrives, like the mistle thrush, they are good sentinels of the garden, issuing an urgent, strident *'pink, pink'* warning. Such a cry is often the initial clue to a cat or sparrowhawk in the vicinity.

♪ 20:18

Through scent, sight, or sound, animals are usually aware of us long before we register their existence. Take the rabbit earlier: our first acknowledgment of them is often their escape – the sudden flight, a bounding leap of legs. At other times, they will simply slink away, while we remain unaware of their presence. To 'clock' them first, you must be very quiet, very still, and they will come to you.

At 20:18, with the light fading, my brain picks up something my eyes have seen, but not exactly crystallised and interpreted, a blurred brown blob, not precisely definitive, hardly an outline – a ghost perhaps? Something tells the brain to check it out, and the eyes work harder, searching for form and movement. The ghost reveals itself as a **muntjac** deer, a doe. How do they do that? No entrance, as if pulled from the very air itself.

Having satisfied herself (wrongly) that no one is about, she stoops her neck, browsing off the newly opening buds of red campion, stopping every few seconds to lift her head, chew, and scan for danger. And she knows, maybe it's my scent, or a twitch of my nose, but she is away, with that muntjac bound, the hooves thudding the floor. Unselfishly, with a warning to others, her white tail, a bigger version of the rabbit scut, flashes the way out of danger. Over the barbed wire fence and out of the garden in one bound, she is away. It will be a few evenings now before she ventures back into the garden.

♪ **20:30**

A blackbird flutters up to the roof of the house and, with the garden now his alone, reminds me why I love him so much. I know I'm being anthropomorphic, but he is pitch-perfect – grander, more confident, clearly pleased with himself. His rivals, nesting beneath the eaves at the back of my shed, are nowhere to be seen or heard. Just this once, it feels as though he sings for the sheer joy of it. This is his 'dusk voice'. Perhaps also for Mrs Blackbird, with the whole garden to themselves.

I'm getting carried away, but a director would happily call out, 'That's a wrap.'

These are deeply special moments in the day, yet I don't begrudge the greenfinch interrupting the maestro with his laid-back, drawn-out wheeze, similar to *'twee-e-er'* – hardly a song by any measure. This greenfinch had a nest earlier, in April, exactly where you'd expect: about eleven feet up, tucked into a piece of evergreen yew growing through a beech hedge. Everything was going well until a magpie stole their young. The nest, curated from horsehair and lined with pigeon feathers, now lies abandoned, slowly gathering debris from the bursting leaf buds all around.

 *Exactly a month later, both these pairs of blackbirds successfully fledged their second broods on 6 June, which is something of a record for me, after their first nests a month earlier in April.*

A woodpigeon coos softly from next door, and following a noisy morning, the garden is gently settling in for the evening.

♪ 20:30

There are three pairs of blackbirds in the garden, and for some reason – I've never quite been able to figure out why – after their calm, 'settling in for the evening' song, they suddenly get panicky, breaking into that nervy *'pink-pink'* call just before going to roost. It's like tucking your child into bed – teeth brushed, all calm – and then giving them a handful of Smarties, for goodness' sake.

The commotion sets off a pheasant across the field, responding with his bolder, more definitive *time-to-go-to-bed* call.

♪ 21:23

It's been a long day, and I'm winding down too – no spink-spink, chaffinch or distant crow, just a quiet realisation that I've had the privilege of seeing and hearing an extraordinary number of creatures in one Wiltshire garden.

A silent silhouette flaps against the western sky above the chestnut tree next door – an apparition, like the muntjac, it drifts from the right – then pauses, hovering. It's a **tawny owl** poised as if to drop on some unseen prey, but strangely, it's high above a tree.

Suddenly, two pigeons explode from the canopy in a clatter of wings. Is it hunting them?

I recently found fresh remains of two stock doves in the garden, their soft light underbelly feathers being picked up by the breeze, while their broken pinions lay scattered in a circle, stiff and inflexible, matted in the grass.

Their small size and the dark patch – which, when the feathers are drawn together, forms that distinctive black wing pattern – make them easy to pick out in flight, or here, just from a single feather, distinguished from the woodpigeons.

These owls are indeed fearsome hunters.

Of all our owls, the tawny, like the badger, is truly nocturnal, and this bird must have been holed up in our dense fir tree. Their old country name is 'brown owl', distinct from the other old country name 'white owl' for the barn owl. They blend seamlessly with tree trunks – their ash-grey streaks, mottled with brown, mirroring the bark's fissures pressed close against their feathers.

Evening is the best time to hear them, and again just before dawn, as they approach their daytime rest, a counterpart to the blackbirds' cycle, the morning song, and the evenings *'clink clink'* to bed.

There is one awe-inspiring, soul-searching, drawn-out *'woo hooooooooooooooooo'*, warning the world to halt, to desist all further activity. 'This is my time.' The blackbirds hunker quietly in the hedge, while the mice twitch, black pools of eyes bulging, on each side of their head.

Time for the night denizens to march forth and for the 'furze cutter' to pack up his bags and head home. We can only pick up the trails in the morning, after the sentinels of sound have criss-crossed the fields, the woods, and flown their aerial pathways.

These audio contrails across the night sky sometimes wake me, especially the short '*seep seep seep*' calls of redwings. On a broad front, they keep up this constant contact – a kind of radar to their chums. Most audible from late October to mid-December, reducing calls continue throughout winter, a reminder of how these birds endlessly roam the countryside in search of food. 'Look up at the stars, look how they shine for you' – (Coldplay) – A lot is going on.

Many passerines migrate at night to avoid predators, reduce overheating, face calmer air, and, of course, help their navigation via the stars. Perhaps that is why you tend to hear them most on misty, claggy nights, when reduced visibility and inevitable disorientation bring them lower to the ground, allowing us to pick up their calls.

In birding and ornithological circles, 'NocMig' is an abbreviation for nocturnal migration monitoring – the study of birds migrating at night by recording their flight calls like an audio version of a trail cam. Using sensitive microphones and recording equipment, this is a mystical part of bird study. It brings me back to the maxim 'To love something you have to understand it'. If you have no idea what a particular sound is, it will probably disappear pretty quickly from your curiosity, slip off the radar. And yet there is so much out there. Taking off at dusk and arriving at their destination just before dawn explains why, as with today, one morning the spotted flycatchers are back and the house martins are here, and on the flip side, the flycatchers have gone – left the previous evening. It all adds to the mystique of ornithology – there is migration, colour, and, of course, these songs.

We love the rawness of birdsong – it's honest, it just is. No one can touch it, no backing singers, no backstory – authenticity in spades. When I recall the birds of my childhood, now lost to agriculture, it is the soundscape that endures most – the skylarks, lapwings, turtle doves, and even the chirpy house sparrows. That happy chatter, from the street corner hedge, the edge of the gutter, a neighbourly gossip – another familiarity gone…

Perhaps that's why we feed ourselves the quick hit of tech, the artificial fertilisers – those packaged bursts of dopamine, the constant drip, drip of TikTok, which rushes in, but dulls the senses. Then a bird sings – and you feel it; for a moment, the world is real again. We like to say we're restoring nature, as if we're the ones holding the reins. The truth is more straightforward: nature restores us, again and again, if we let it in.

Traditional schooling often separates us from nature, contributing to societal disconnection from the natural world, which in turn leads to higher stress levels and anxiety. We should embed nature more deeply into our core educational systems and ground ourselves once more with the sparrow on the gutter.

There was no 'NocMig' tonight. The tawny owl ushered in a hushed, black stillness.

Creatures will be afoot, but they are now closed from me in their nightly wanderings.

PART
THREE

Bullfinch

ROUND-UP OF THE DAY
What did we find?

What didn't we see that we might have expected, and what caught us by surprise?

The No-shows

Most days, a **raven** or two flies overhead, always one way, south to north, which I never understand – when do they go back? That unmistakable deep-throated *'kronk kronk'*, keeping them in constant communication with their fellow brethren even as they fly. They fought earlier in the year with our pair of buzzards, competing for a nest platform in the

Scots pines at the end of the garden. Or to be more precise, one specific branch, which overhangs well into the field by a good ten yards. The commotion brought me out of the house, but the buzzards eventually won.

A raven's beak, a massive weapon, makes their head look bigger than it really is. Intelligent birds plundering the fields at the top of the corvid gang, not much gives way to them. They are doing well, very well, too well for some sheep farmers.

Goldcrests were here earlier in the year, with their distinctive high-pitched repetitive *'zee, zee, zee'*, or *'zi, zi, zi'* as they hunt among their favourite pine trees, especially the larches. Like the long-tailed tits, they keep up a constant chatter except for when the male spins up the same notes with increasing intensity, ending in a flourish *'zi-zi-zi-zi-zeee-zeeee'*.

There is often a **green woodpecker** searching for ants on the lawn. If you look closely, you will find the holes in the soil where they repeatedly stick their long, probing, sticky tongue to snare their favourite food of ants. Sometimes in July, they bring their slightly dowdy young ones to teach them how to forage. But more often than not, you hear their 'yaffle' as they rock up to a tree, a wild, echoing laugh like a hurried *'klu, klu, klu, klu'* spat out from a tree trunk. Is there a witch cackling in the garden, a woodland spirit?

Although already here this summer in Marlborough town centre, we may have been just a tad early for the local **swifts** that nest in crevices under the eaves of the local Kennet Valley Primary School. It was not until 18 May that the first one flew over the house. I have tried to attract them to our home with a wooden nest box and even built three brick swift boxes into the fabric of the house, all to no avail. I suspect there is not enough of a drop to make them interested. However, not to waste the real estate, pied wagtails and blue tits have subsequently used them.

A **barn owl** was always a possibility of a sighting on 6 May, especially since we were up before dawn. They are relatively common here in Wiltshire. We often hear their eerie, drawn-out, two-second *'shreee'* as they launch, outstretched, their talon-tipped legs at some terrified mouse in the garden.

The next day, 7 May a **jay** flapped its clumsy flight – another bird that vanishes for much of the year until it is acorn time and they then appear everywhere.

Two **collared doves** which don't show that day are regular visitors. These delicate birds with their soft, almost pink colour in the right light, first bred in the UK as recently as 1955 in Norfolk.

They are now spread nationally, and a pair lives as far north as the garden of *The Ulbster Arms* in Halkirk, Caithness, just shy of the Orkney Isles. They have a straightforward repetitive three-note call:

'*coo- COO- coo*' or the football chant '*U-NI-ted*' easily distinguishable from the deeper, longer five-note call of the woodpigeon which says:

'*coo COO, coo, coo, coo*' or '*You two fools, you two!*'

It is tempting to think the collared doves have taken over the ecological niche vacated by the steeply declining turtle dove, but they are more a bird of the garden than the 'turtles' which live in the fields.

The Surprise Appearences

The **cuckoo** must be the standout. Like a meteor it arrived and was gone before you could blink. I've never seen one before in my garden, and I rarely hear them locally. Yet this bird – having left the Congo sometime in April, chose, whether by accident or design, within a total UK landmass of some 243,610 km^2, to pass on its migration just above head-height here, precisely here, at Latitude 51.409798°N and Longitude 1.79027°W. Amazing!

A **bullfinch** is always a joy to see – especially as, for the second year running, they have chosen to nest in the garden. It's one of those birds that makes you feel you must be doing something right if it graces you with its presence.

I like to think we encouraged the **kestrel**, with our abundance of voles, mice, and shrews. They were virtually the only bird of prey I would see as a child, yet they seem less common now. I can't help but feel they are being pushed out by larger, more assertive raptors such as buzzards and red kites, and by competition with the growing numbers of jackdaws for nesting holes.

The tally of our day 6 May is recorded on the BTO Birdtrak website for citizen science.

Fifty percent of the 'Dawn Chorus' birds were first recorded between 04:35 and 05:58, and all the song birds by 07:46.

This is the list of birds I recorded. I also recorded rabbit, fox, muntjac, stoat, brimstone, painted lady butterflies, and numerous bumble bees.

Species	Time first seen/heard
Robin	04:35
Blackbird	04:36
Jackdaw, Pheasant, Pigeon	04:37
Heron	04:38
Blackcap	04:50
Carrion crow	04:51
Wren	05:00
Goldfinch	05:04
Chaffinch	05:12
Rook	05:14
Great tit	05:15

Species	Time first seen/heard
Song thrush	05:26
Mistle thrush	05:30
Stock dove	05:38
Spotted flycatcher	05:40
Blue tit	05:42
Greenfinch	05:44
Magpie	05:45
Tree creeper	05:54
Dunnock	05:55
Chiffchaff	06:23
House martin	06:26
Mallard	06:27
Pied wagtail	06:35
Coal tit	06:40
Long-tailed tit	06:44
Cuckoo	07:00
Red kite	07:01
Bullfinch	07:15
Starling	07:43
Swallow	07:46
Nuthatch	15:10
Kestrel	15:40
Lesser black back gull	16:12
Canada goose	20:05
Tawny owl	21:23

PART
FOUR

Thrush nest

MY GARDEN NESTING ROUND-UP 2025

6 May, the day of our sighting and sound recording of all the birds in my garden, was particularly successful because the garden serves as a prime habitat for many nesting birds. Here, I take a closer look at the various species I recorded nesting throughout that whole year, and provide suggestions on how you can encourage them to nest in your garden.

There were 62 nesting attempts, at least that I know of – I will always miss some – with 22 individual species, 44 successful fledglings, and 19 failures.

Tally of my garden nests 2025

Goldcrest – one attempt: one failure

Treecreeper – one attempt: one success

Bullfinch – one attempt: one success

Buzzard – one attempt: one success

Blue tit – one attempt: one success

Great tit – one attempt: one success

Coal tit – one attempt: one success

Chiffchaff – one attempt: one failure

Swallow – two attempts: one success, one failure

Long-tailed tit – two attempts: one success, one failure

Greenfinch – two attempts: one success, one failure

Mistle thrush – two attempts: one success, one failure

Spotted flycatcher – three attempts: two successes, one failure

Pied wagtail – three attempts: two successes, one failure

Dunnock – three attempts: one success, two failures

Robin – four attempts: three successes, one failure

Stock dove – four attempts: two successes, two failures

Blackbird – five attempts: five successes

House martin – five attempts: five successes

Goldfinch – six attempts: three successes, three failures

Woodpigeon – six attempts: three successes, three failures

Jackdaw – eight attempts: eight successes

Starting first from the bottom of the chart, the most numerous bird nests were those of the **jackdaw**. Not the best neighbour for nesting songbirds, but this is how we get along.

They are attracted by the epicormic growths (weak clusters of shoots sprouting on a tree's trunk) in the lime trees at the end of the garden. Hidden in a treetop skyscraper, they generally exit straight out across the fields to feed, and crucially, not over the garden. I once tried to reduce these dense clusters of small branches growing midway up the trunk, but stopped upon revealing a mass of mummified bats, old eggs, stock dove remains, and general dried bird shit. It is an ecosystem in its own right. And so I am destined to have a colony of jackdaws forever at the bottom of the garden.

They play an interesting role as a food source (at least for the young fledglings) for both buzzards and tawny owls, which in turn feed their own young on baby jackdaws. Come fledging time, I have counted up to twelve piles of black feathers where a silent night attack by tawny owls or a noisy daytime raid by buzzards has been their undoing. Among the jackdaws also nest stock doves who share the same fate.

No surprise that the following most dominant species is the **woodpigeon**, which nests openly in low elder, dogwood, and creepers around the house, as well as in our beech and yew hedges. They leave themselves, plus their eggs and chicks, quite exposed to the tawny owls and buzzards. I come down in the morning, and there is a pile of feathers on the ground and no eggs in the nest. It's a larder, a live butchers' stall. One reason for the pigeons' abundance is their ability to nest late into the autumn. Several nests were still present in September.

Our most common songbird, the **goldfinch**, attempted six nests, with a fifty percent success rate. The remaining nests were all fairly exposed and subsequently predated. Do the birds learn? Do they get wiser at hiding their nests? It is savage in the garden in spring.

My greatest reward that year came from the **house martins**. For years now, great spotted woodpeckers have been chiselling into the martins' mud domes to predate eggs and chicks. A well-intentioned and well-stocked winter bird table encourages the woodpeckers, but not without unintended summer consequences, so now, no more peanuts. This trend of woodpecker attacks, if it continues, will be devastating to the already declining martin population, as great spotted woodpeckers have increased by 378% since 1967, according to the BTO. To mitigate this problem, I have attached solid woodcrete martin nest boxes, which are more resistant to the woodpeckers' attacks. The problem seems most intense just before and just after the young woodpeckers fledge, when they are at their most demanding of the parents in terms of food.

It was 'happy days' throughout June, July, and August – a constant turn of wings around the house, the martins' dark feathers accentuating their bold white rumps, as they acrobatically sought insects. They seem to seek your presence, fill your windows with chatter and your skies with boundless purpose, in your face, but never ask anything of you except a sheltered eave to spend their summer days. Should we deign to open our ears and eyes, they represent everything nature brings to our hearts.

On 30 August, I counted one hundred martins swarming around the house and settling among the nests, roof, and brickwork. What were they doing? It only lasted half an hour, but it was an incredible natural spectacle; they came to me right here in the garden. What were they doing? I think they were creating a sense of place, an imprint for next year, a good home to return to. It's a lovely thought.

By early September, most had left, but in a freshening breeze, with the odd leaf hurtling off the trees, the few remaining martins weave their imaginary hunts above my head, free and unaware of the deep thoughts I have on the ground below. As night falls, they rise up and up together, a tight flock of some fifty individuals, all the while chattering. Below at garden height, singles of swallows trickle through heading west, about one every minute.

The next morning, just silent bare horizons. My thoughts are lost in their departure, with empty skies until the next time… next year.

When **siting nest boxes**, for all birds, not just house martins, consider the aspect and height. East is best, the early morning sun warms the nest, moving round to the south before it becomes too overpowering, and crucially, it remains sheltered from the prevailing westerly winds and accompanying rain. All four of our house martin nest boxes were used this year on our east gable with a clear drop from the eaves across the lawn. Cover is often neglected, leaving boxes exposed to the elements and predators. Birds need peace to nest successfully.

This was also the best year I have known for **blackbird** nests, with earlier than usual first fledglings by 16 April. This helped some pairs double brood, with one pair of blackbirds using the same nest three times, which is highly unusual.

I was fortunate to be on hand when one of the third brood tumbled from the nest. Placing it back, I found little more remained than a rough platform of flattened, matted material. Yet, set snugly in the corner of two adjoining walls, they could retreat, huddled nervously for shelter against the wooden planks, their crouched eyes watching.

Most small birds – including blackbirds – build a new nest for each brood, and for good reasons.

Nest hygiene
An old nest can quickly become a haven for mites, fleas, and other tiny parasites. Left unchecked, these intruders pose a serious threat to the chicks' health. By crafting a new home, the parents offer their young a clean, fresh start in which to grow.

Structural integrity
The nests themselves are fragile works of art, built from twigs, mud, grass, and other fleeting materials. After a brood has fledged and the nest has endured sun, wind, and rain, it rarely remains sturdy enough to cradle another clutch. A fresh nest ensures that the next generation is supported safely.

Predator avoidance
A used nest carries the scent of its former inhabitant, or an advertising stream of excrement, smell, and visual reminders to prowling predators. By building anew – often nearby but in a subtly different corner – parents reduce the risk of discovery, giving their chicks a better chance to survive.

That I witnessed three successful broods of blackbirds in a single nest was highly unusual, a testament to the many abandoned nests from previous broods and past years dotted throughout the garden.

A bird, I am sure often simply mistaken as a pigeon, somewhere in size between a woodpigeon and a collared dove, is the **stock dove**. Like their cousins, they enjoy a long breeding season, and their fragile nests here are placed in the relative safety of the lime tree epicormic, at the bottom of the garden. They too fall victim to the tawny owl and buzzard, their pure white eggs symmetrically oval, just broken shells littering the ground, hijacking your stare from the bare earth and feathers all around.

There were four **robin** nests with a double brood for two pairs and, like the blackbirds, the first nest successfully fledged early by 23 April. Now all summer, one youngster shadowed me around the vegetable garden – his upright stance and habit of snatching a morsel before flitting to a perch marked him out as a robin, yet his speckled feathers would have otherwise been misleading. By the middle of August, his post-juvenile moult signalled his impending adulthood, as each feather, each speckle by speckle, was pushed into the flotsam of time. Bedraggled, a slight hue of blue appeared around his cheeks, and blotches of red began to stain his breast. For post adolescent robins, this stage is more than just a coming of age – he would now need to put his best foot forward, an adult fighting bird to defend this territory for the winter, or die.

He never reached that zenith. His adolescent world, his garden haven, lulled him into a false sense of security. An aerial assault smashed his cranium, instantly squeezing any squeak of protest, a few more speckles on the breeze to join the flotsam. The sparrowhawk had nabbed him, right in front of my eyes, off my very own back doorstep. Damn.

One leg dangled the lifeless form, swinging it right and left among the trees, the hawk escaping like a cheetah with its kill, before settling down to dine, to pick to the bone. Born, raised, and eaten within a tiny circle of life, a small horizon, no wider than a few trees.

This brings me to the **dunnock**, with three nests, and I am sure I will find more once the leaves fall to the ground. When nesting, it is one of our shyest birds. It will not sit quietly when you check the hedges, but creeps out of the nest through the branches and away, long before you spy the mossy cup. Similarly, when returning, it will skirt its way along the ground, never flying directly to the nest, even when the young are at their hungriest.

They only draw attention to themselves when singing or chasing the females across the grass with fluttering, fawning flaps of their wings, but even here they are never far from cover. It is an unfair comparison – for after all, they are a songbird – but like rats keeping a few hairs brushing the skirting board, they keep a few feathers in touch with a hedge or bush. Where they excel is in the blueness of their eggs, a wonder borne from the drabness of this underwhelming 'little brown job' of a bird.

In complete contrast, the nesting **pied wagtails** flaunted their presence. Two-tone in colour, with the constant flicking of the tail and their two syllable *'chi-sic'*, I could almost touch their first nest from my office window. It was so typical of wagtails that they liked to reach it on foot by running along the roof.

Evolution has taught them this approach, but unlike the dunnocks, they were always conspicuous. Even with beaks packed full of insects, waiting for you to take only two steps further away before feeding their young, they never ceased their bobbing tails and two-tone calls. Often in the evening, when the clamour for food had died down, one of the parents would take to sitting on the apex of the roof, relieved that the job for the day was done. It was at this point, with one adult finally relaxed, guard down, and exposed on the roof, I feared Mr. or Mrs. Sparrowhawk might come hurtling over the building. I need not have worried, and the wagtails joined the house martins as my chattering companions all summer.

In joint ninth place, with two nest successes and one failure, is that gem of a bird, the **spotted flycatcher**. A most understated and underestimated little brown bird. We are graced to have their presence here each year, 'old established gardens' being their preference, but invariably they nest on our 'old established house'.

Spotted flycatchers (*Muscicapa striata*) have experienced a significant decline in the UK, with a reduction of around 85% in their population since the 1970s. I fret about their return each spring, I seek them out because they enchant me, and they are thriving under the safety umbrella of our garden. Elegant but drab, modest and restrained, these mousy brown birds love to sit on the guttering of the house. If you don't look, you will not see. This is not a creature that pokes you in the eye; you must seek it out. They may have nested in your garden without you noticing this last summer. Perhaps you'll stumble upon one of their old nests while pruning creepers and roses on the house, and you'll think nothing of it.

As the young begin developing their wing pinions, they peer out from their nursery, frantically watching for a returning parent with a beak full of insects. This is optimum flycatcher watching time as the parents show off their hunting skills in the evening garden, all about wings, flight, death, and providing food.

One June evening, all four adults filled the sky at once, pirouetting and darting like mayflies. Every so often came the sharp snap of a beak, and when they paused to perch, their heads swiveled owl-like, weighing up which of the airborne morsels would offer the greatest reward. And when they find that perfect fly, they will chase and harry it like a hobby.

They have their favourite hunting perches: the metal obelisk with the sweet peas, a bare branch in the larch tree, all the guttering around the house and various sarsen stones we have dotted around the garden. Key is an open area, with good visibility but close to cover. On windy and wet days, they will hunt closer to the ground and find shelter on the leeward side of the house, where the insects are still active.

I was fortunate this year to witness three chicks on their maiden flights. The first flew into my office window, alerting me to the event, before it wobbled its way to a large beech tree a good twenty metres away. Another flew twenty metres out of the nest to a birch tree and I saw a third erratically make its way thirty metres to a large line of lime trees. An instinctive scattering, a final release from the parental pressures of having 'all ones' eggs in the same basket'.

Once the initial flight is over, the fledgling flycatchers sit still, making a high-pitched and loud '*tssp*' to let their parents know where they are. However, it is tough for us humans to pinpoint the exact source of these calls.

This leads me to the third crucial element for their success, at the critical point of fledging: the sanctuary of large trees, safe from predators and sheltered from wind and rain, while they hone their flight muscles and feeding skills.

On the west side of the house, a flycatcher nest entwined in honeysuckle failed this year. It was vulnerable – either to rats, which could easily scale the six-foot height, or to a passing corvid, since it was very visible. In addition, the parent looked miserable, panting as she endured the afternoon sun and cold when exposed to rain and wind.

Books on ornithology describe the spotted flycatcher's preferred habitats as large mature gardens, but if that is not you, don't be put off. As long as you have some nearby large trees, you can make a difference. Construct a small platform, or attach a swallow box to a building, sheltered from above, with a commanding view. Hopefully, this understated and underestimated little brown bird will grace your summer evenings.

At least two pairs of **greenfinches** nested in the garden this year. They are our only truly 'green' bird, apart from the larger green woodpecker and the ring-necked parakeets who have successfully extended their march west along the Thames valley from their stronghold in the London parks. I know, however, that when the leaves are blown from the hedges later in the year, it will reveal more greenfinch nests that escaped my notice.

While there were two attempted **mistle thrush** nests this year, with one success and one failure, I am confident it was the same pair, and I covered their nesting habits earlier on pages 31-32 of this book. Once the pair has finished nesting, they disappear locally, not to return until early autumn in preparation for the cycle to start all over again. Where do they go? I would love to know. In Scotland, I have watched flocks of fifty strong in August, but here only a few ever appear at once. Still, as with so much else in the garden, my heart lifts a little each time I hear and see their return.

Two pairs of **long-tailed tits** nested this year, with one success and one failure. The failure came with the death of one of the parents, who I found lying on the ground. There were no marks, no scratches, and it seemed in good health, cradled in my hands.

When the band of eight or so birds at the bird table dwindled to just a pair at a time, I knew they must be nesting nearby. Building a nest – sometimes from hundreds of feathers, with lichen and spider silk woven in – takes time. Time to watch – time well spent to see where they go. Sometimes you get lucky, as with the chiffchaff and the feather in her beak. More often, though, it's their ceaseless gathering of spider webs that gives them away, prompting you to say – 'Here we go,' and follow their straight yet undulating flight to a new home, usually hidden deep within a thorny bush or hedge.

Although the house martins have done well, I worry about 'our' **swallows**. At least they raised one successful brood this year, although I am unsure as to what happened to the second brood. A few years back, the four houses adjacent to each other, and a stable where we live, all had a pair of swallow nests each year. That is five pairs reduced to one. Nothing obvious points to a change in local conditions or a change in habitat, which are common causes of decline. As a long-range migrant traveling some 6,000 miles from southern Africa, perhaps more erratic weather patterns along the way are the challenge. I love spotting their looping liquid flight among the more haphazard, less spontaneous flight of the house martins.

In late July, perhaps one hundred strong were congregated on some telephone wires overhanging the

River Kennet. Now these are thought to be the first broods migrating earlier, while the parents stay on for a second brood. Indeed, the tail feathers appeared shorter than those of a fully grown adult, so maybe the theory is true.

It was not until September that another group of five birds appeared at 07:30, only to have increased to ten by 7:40. At 08:00, there were twenty, and then they all left in one go. Were they waiting for the air to warm, and were they collecting birds early on so they could migrate together?

This year, I found a **chiffchaff's** nest in the garden for the first time. I was in deep 'cuckoo' mode – sitting quietly, watching what was going on. This is how cuckoos find nests to parasitise – sit quietly, and nature will come to you. Small songbirds, in particular, rarely see humans as a serious threat. It was the white pigeon feather in her bill that first caught my eye. Peripheral vision added to my senses. The nest really is like they show in the books – a dome of dried grass barely a foot off the ground, wrapped in the base of some yew hedge and sheltered in front by the growing cow parsley – another example of a rough piece of ground left to its own device.

The single **coal tit** nest we had in the old drainpipe, I have written about in a previous chapter. Every year, coal tits investigate this habitat, but this is the first time I have proved beyond doubt complete occupation. It will be interesting to see if it's used again next year and if so, how long the drainpipe dynasty continues.

While the coal and blue tits can be quite adventurous in their nesting locations, I always find that the great tits prefer a simple, traditional nest box, again placed on the east side of a building or tree.

With only one **blue tit** nest in the garden, this was their lowest nesting attempt in fifteen years. There are usually at least three nests in or around the house, one in the garage and one in a nest box.

There were plenty of adults around in the spring, and good weather, as seen by the success of all the other species. My only hypothesis is that the normal nooks and crannies were full of parasites after the mild winter, and they decided to nest elsewhere. Note to self – I should put up some new boxes this coming year and thoroughly clean any existing nests.

A pair of **buzzards** raised a solitary chick this year, and as I write these lines now in September, the chick is still filling the garden with its grating, jarring, piercing, and yes, really whining screech – *'Kee-ah, kee-ah, kee-ah'* and on and on it goes. This is not the gentle, sometimes soporific 'mewing' of an adult buzzard. The poor parents are nowhere near the old nest, sat hunched three hundred yards away from this plaintive begging demand for food.

I am not so lucky.

A strong reason for planting mixed hedges in the garden is that a greater variety of plants increases the chances of attracting a wider range of animals. So, like the greenfinches I spoke of earlier, a pair of **bullfinches**, similar to last year, successfully raised a brood in a hawthorn hedge where it grows up through some beech. One plant can make all the difference. Again, similar to the greenfinches, they nest high up, say four metres on the edge of the hedge – always the edge.

What amazes me about bullfinch nests is how quickly the young grow that unmistakable stout bill, easily identifying them as bullfinches early on. They stayed around the garden for a few days after fledging, sitting quietly in the vegetable garden. You would first be alerted to them by their '*diu diu*'.

Then one, then two, and then three of these wonderful birds flew in boldly, looking for weed seeds among the carrots, beetroot, and beans. Their colours mimicked the adults, but in more washed watercolours, still very distinguishable as bullfinches by the prominent white rump and black wing bars. They are the definition of 'birds of a feather flock together' – they have no time for other birds.

Now, the **treecreeper** was a nest I did not find, but the fledglings in the garden were as wobbly as could be and had just left a nest somewhere close by. Where? My suspicion is they nested in a crevice in one of the old pollard lime trees – they only need a small opening in which they can wedge their nest. It's tough to find, and the parents' habit of feeding high up in the trees' branches doesn't make it any easier. The best chance to observe is when treecreepers fly down to the base of a tree before starting their ascent, searching for food in the trunk. These young had not yet mastered the art of tree climbing, which is their destiny, and would cling for dear life to the vertical branches, preferring to attempt a weak flight rather than creep up the bark like their parents.

Now for the very last of the 21 garden nesters of summer 2025 – the **goldcrest**. My only reference was the tiny moss and lichen ball, no bigger than a tennis ball, lying strewn on the grass below a large leylandii tree. The remains of a robbery, a shattered home discovered, raided, and discarded. This often happens to the first goldcrest nests, and later broods are more successful. Like the treecreepers, it is more often the sound of the birds high up in the trees that draws them to your attention.

The goldcrest is our smallest British bird, weighing just five to seven grams – barely more than a twenty pence piece of feathers, flesh, and claw. In comparison, our buzzard, our largest nesting bird, weighs in at a giant 1.4kg, approximately 280 times the weight of the goldcrest. Maybe it was the buzzard that found the nest, but I would put that probability sixth behind jackdaw, magpie, squirrel, jay, or carrion crow.

PART FIVE

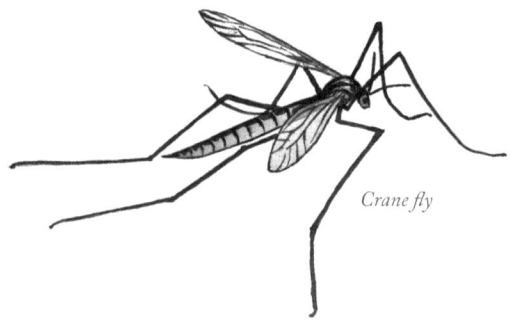

Crane fly

THE INCONVENIENT TRUTHS

Forty-plus bird species in a single day is a pretty good tally, but it is not a coincidence. Nor were the toads, frogs, grass snakes, lizards, butterflies, moths, bees, voles, mice, and a whole heap of invertebrates that I struggle to identify.

I attribute this abundance to three habitat factors:

INSECTS – no chemicals
SHELTER – little disturbance
SAFETY – some predator control

Have we got our conservation top-down focus the wrong way round, and should it be bottom-up?

We should have an RSPI (Royal Society for the Protection of Insects). Would we then need the RSPB (Royal Society for the Protection of Birds)? What if we channelled some of their millions into insect revival? Now I am being deliberately provocative, but *'give everything an insect'* might be a better slogan than the bird box campaign *'give everything a home'*.

While welcome in principle, *'give everything a home'* can feel little more than a marketing drive to sell more bird boxes, which are all too often poorly sited in direct sunlight or in the prevailing winds and rain, in over-tidy, sterile gardens consumed with disturbance and the 'clack clack' of the 'find me a bird nest, find me a happy magpie'.

I recently spent some time fishing in Caithness, right at the very north of Scotland, where you can see the Orkney Isles across the sea. The abundance of starlings, swifts, swallows, sand and house martins, and numerous meadow pipits, was way above anything here in Wiltshire, but then there is plenty of permanent pasture, filled with crane flies. In your garden, ask yourself a simple question: how can I increase the insect population?

We are in a conservation doom loop, where we devote all our efforts to predator introduction. I am as happy as anyone to see a majestic red kite soaring over the garden, a pine marten crossing the path when I am fishing in Scotland, or a sea eagle slowly flapping past me on north Uist, while I fish the wild sea lochs. Still, what have these particular animals ever done for conservation – I mean real conservation? Yes, they are lovely to see, but let's be honest, are they really the holy grail of the trophic cascade?

What actual benefits do they bring to our ecosystems? Apart from the wow factor?

I visited a guillemot colony on the outer edge of Loch Broom in western Scotland. As the rib neared the cliffs, you could see the familiar white stains of years of fish-filled bird shite staining the rocks, but the ledges were empty, utterly devoid of nesting birds in May. My boat guide casually informed me that the sea eagles had spent years harassing the birds, and that the guillemots and shags had now dispersed. Even more interesting, the sea eagles too had abandoned their eyrie themselves this year, presumably due to a lack of food.

The **sea eagle** is a large bird, and anecdotal evidence suggests they drive golden eagles away from their territories. Simple question: why challenge our not-so-common existing golden eagle population?

Salmon fishing in Iceland in September, I asked why there was a magnificent yellow hi vis scarecrow on top of a cliff in the absolute middle of nowhere. *'Oh, it's to scare the sea eagles from predating the salmon spawning in the redds below.'*

This raises two issues:

1. We don't have so many pools stuffed with spawning salmon these days in the UK, so we are reintroducing sea eagles to a very different land than they would have encountered two hundred years ago, and they are going to need to find other food sources.

2. Our Atlantic salmon are now IUCN red-listed in the UK, so why bring back one of their main predators?

The same question applies to the **pine marten**, another fantastic predator, which may ultimately be the final straw for our few remaining capercaillie, as pine martens prey on the nests. They have been reintroduced to Dartmoor, where ground-nesting waders such as curlew, redshank, and snipe are already on a trend to oblivion – why do this? The story is told that they will hunt down grey squirrels, but at what cost to all the other wildlife…

When discussing Dartmoor, there is even talk of reintroducing the **wildcat**. Given that the demise of the wildcat is primarily due to interbreeding with domestic cats, it seems the impact will be an increase in the feral cat population on Dartmoor. This is not only pointless but also reckless.

Then the **lynx**, which we are promised will reduce badger and fox populations. Why would they hunt another carnivore when they have sheep served on a plate, and a summer to gorge on roe deer calves? Lynx are solitary creatures, with a requirement for vast territories of up to 1,200 sq km for some males. I doubt this will have much of an impact on the local deer population.

The red kite is a notable example of a successful reintroduction, and they are indeed lovely to see. However, has any impact study been conducted to assess how they have affected the breeding success of ground-nesting birds, such as skylarks?

Once a predator is reintroduced, it is a one-way street, and we have no way to turn back the clock or implement any form of population control.

I have nothing against all these reintroduced apex creatures, but I do think we are barking up the wrong tree and wasting precious time and money.

We should first focus our conservation efforts from the bottom up by supporting the invertebrates at the bottom of the food chain, and consider preserving bio-abundance before striving to increase biodiversity.

This approach will have a more dramatic effect as it works its way up the food chain, rather than relying on a top-down strategy of introducing more apex and mesopredators.

We are not Yellowstone Park. We are a small island with seventy-odd million people, and growing, which does not have the space for large predators, nor the habitat to support them.

People fall in love with big, charismatic things, which helps fuel public funding. So, the NGOs keep pushing them – it's the golden ticket. Anything that gets in their way is bad. And by the way, there is no recourse if 'big animal' introductions have a negative impact. Once established, the genie is out of the bottle. Always top down, becomes the mantra.

Our screens, whether Instagram, TikTok, Facebook, YouTube or television, are all filled with magnificent predators, as if these are the only animals in town, while pastoral scenes are filled with sheep, and acres of green wheat – lands now shorn of ground-nesting birds.

What are we doing about the plight of our common birds, which have seen drastic declines?

For example, approximate declines since the 1970s:

Starlings: 80%+

Skylark: 60%

House sparrow: 60%

We gloss over these 'lbj's' (little brown jobs) because they fail to capture the public's imagination. The agenda is driven by marketing, money, and the ever-increasing need to subsidise the payroll.

But they are the canaries in the coal mine.

According to UK Pet Food (the industry body), over half of UK households feed wild birds, and the wild bird food market was estimated at approximately £380 million in 2023 – an increase of £35 million from the previous year. What a lovely country we are. **But a safe nesting habitat and insects for chicks are often lacking.** Those very same seed eaters that come to your bird table in the winter primarily feed their young on insects and insect larvae in the spring.

Let's take a moment to look at the definition of red-listed UK birds.
• they have declined by more than 50% in the last 25 years, or longer.
• they are globally threatened or are not recovering from historical decline.
• they have had their breeding range in the UK reduced drastically by at least 50% in the last 25 years or longer.
This is sobering stuff.

Of the 71 red-listed species below, well over half, 47, rely directly on insects to survive. Let alone indirectly. At the same time, a further twenty depend directly or indirectly on the bottom of the food chain in our coastal waters.

Bottom up, our focus should be on the bottom up.

Figures taken from British Trust for Ornithology/Joint Nature Conservation Committee Bird Trends Report of red-listed UK birds. Last updated 31 May 2024

Arctic Skua

Balearic Shearwater

Bewick's Swan

Black Grouse

Blacktailed Godwit

Capercaillie

Cirl Bunting

Common Gull

Common Scoter

Corn Bunting

Corncrake

Cuckoo

Curlew

Dotterel

Dunlin

Fieldfare

Goldeneye

Grasshopper Warbler

Great Black-backed Gull

Great Skua

Greenfinch

Grey Partridge

Hawfinch

Hen Harrier

Herring Gull

House Martin

House Sparrow

Kittiwake

Lapwing

Leach's Storm Petrel

Lesser Spotted Woodpecker

Linnet

Long-tailed Duck
Marsh Tit
Marsh Warbler
Merlin
Mistle Thrush
Montagu's Harrier
Pochard
Puffin
Purple Sandpiper
Ptarmigan
Redbacked Shrike
Redpoll
Rednecked Grebe
Rednecked Phalarope
Ring Ouzel
Ringed Plover
Roseate Tern
Ruff
Savi's Warbler

Shag
Skylark
Smew
Slavonian Grebe
Spotted Flycatcher
Starling
Swift
Tree Pipit
Tree Sparrow
Twite
Velvet Scoter
Whimbrel
Whinchat
Whitefronted Goose
Willow Tit
Wood Warbler
Woodcock
Yellow Wagtail
Yellowhammer

Insects for wildlife
Inconvenient truth No 1:
You need a chemical-free garden.

This is perhaps the most important aspect I can recommend. In our garden we have no pesticides or weedkillers.

There is a wealth of chemical-free opportunity in your lawn, a permanent pasture that can mitigate much of the sterile arable landscape we see all around us. Countryside Stewardship farming is leading the way in agriculture – don't become left behind in your garden.

'*Oh, look at those lovely daisies in the lawn,*' people exclaim in wonder, and then they carry on creating their monotone, green monoculture deserts. **I love my lawn, but I am not a slave to it.**

Mowing the lawn is an adventure, creating paths, and, through nature, painting colours with rich mediums of oils, watercolours, pencils, and pastels. My job is to manage the competition between the flowers and grasses, determining how often they should be cut and at what height. Some flowers I do not cut from May to September – while others, like daisies and clover, I need to keep short, where the green woodpeckers can feed in comfort.

By September my lawn is a fresh green, but all summer, it hummed with bees, rasped with grasshoppers, and became a home for cinnabar caterpillars, the common blue and small copper, while pyramid orchids appeared from nowhere. A rich tapestry of white, yellow, and purple flowers evolved throughout the summer, and yes, I did remove any thistles, and kept in check some of the dandelions.

White Lawn Flowers
Daisy
Chickweed – Common
Chickweed – Mouse Ear
Clover – White
Yarrow

Yellow Lawn Flowers
Black medic
Bird's foot Trefoil
Buttercup – Bulbous
Cat's-ear
Celandine
Dandelion
Hawkbit
Hawks-Beard
Mouse-ear Hawkweed
Ragwort

Red/Purple/Mauve/Blue Lawn Flowers
Selfheal
Violet

How to mow for wildlife

So what does my mowing regime actually look like?

No Mow May is full of good intentions – but what then happens in June? The exuberance of May can produce a thick sward, capable of swamping the more delicate wildflowers you are trying to encourage. For that reason, I mow until around the third week of May – longer if the spring is wet and growth particularly strong.

From then on, some blocks are left uncut through to September, allowing flowers to rise above the grasses. Between them, I mow paths – the fun part – beloved of clover and daisies, and accompanied by blackbirds, starlings, robins, dunnocks, and, as already mentioned, green woodpeckers.

What you are creating is a mosaic: edges and transitions, small habitats within what appears to be a simple lawn. It then takes about three cuts in September to bring the lawn back to a manageable level. Don't worry if it looks a little brown at first; it will soon green over with the autumn rains. It's important to continue mowing until winter so that, come spring, your mower doesn't face a tangle of long, wet grass.

Lawns take time to shed the excess nutrients that have built up over the years, nutrients that have turned so many of our 'green' spaces into miniature silage fields. But with patience and careful management – paths mown, blocks left to flower, cutting timed to growth – you can transform even a nutrient-rich lawn into a living mosaic: a tapestry of flowers, grasses, and insects, alive with birdsong and movement, quietly restoring balance to the land.

After three annual cuts, the lawn is prepared for winter. The green woodpecker is back searching for ants, and soon the migrant blackbirds from Scandinavia will be listening – heads tilted for earthworms. Some moss will grow, keeping it green through the darker months, but by April next year, the moss will be outcompeted by grass and flowers.

Organic vegetable growing

A chemical-free vegetable garden can be challenging, but it becomes all the more rewarding when the harvest is for our own table, while insect netting protects brassicas from both large and small white caterpillars.

Most aphid infestations will resolve themselves naturally, but if they persist, remove and destroy heavily affected plants. These plants are often inherently weaker – and slugs instinctively target vulnerable plants.

A sharp pair of scissors is a quick and humane defence against slugs and snails. Simple jam jars filled with beer, dug level into the vegetable beds, do work – but it's best to start early in the year, before sowing and planting out, so the slug population doesn't get a head start.

Building resilience against this natural susceptibility is key. The answer lies in healthy soil, rich in microbes that help plants absorb essential minerals and retain moisture. Entire books have been written on the subject, particularly by proponents of the 'no-dig' method, such as Charles Dowding, alongside the importance of creating and using your own compost.

Shelter to protect the birds
Inconvenient truth No 2:
The disturbance our pets cause.
Wildlife grows accustomed to humans when we repeatedly pose no threat. But a cat is *always* a predator, and even a friendly dog – though it may not directly kill – can cause stress and dispersal away from your garden. Disturbance is probably our most underestimated and least understood cause of wildlife decline, because it's a silent, invisible disruption.

The degree to which eggs cool, if left unattended, and die during incubation depends on the species and the ambient temperature.

For small passerines, this could be as little as fifteen minutes, at temperatures of less than 10°C, and as much as two hours at higher temperatures around 20°C. While larger birds such as ducks, especially in well-insulated nests, may live much longer, I would guess most of your garden birds are the smaller type!

The other unintended consequence is a higher risk of predation, as the parents leave the nests unguarded.

Key factors influencing egg survival when parents are pushed off the nest

- **Embryo development stage:** Early-stage embryos are more sensitive.
- **Nest insulation:** Grass, leaves and feathers all help to retain heat.
- **Ambient outside temperature**
- **Disturbance frequency:** Repeated exposure increases cooling risk.

Current estimates put the UK's dog and cat population at around 13 million each. Over the past fifteen years, the number of dogs has risen by approximately 34%, while the number of cats has increased by about 7%. That means some **26 million** four-legged friends now roam our gardens – and that has consequences. We have neither a cat nor a dog; that is our choice, but I am sure it contributes to our abundant garden wildlife, especially with the shyer animals such as grass snakes, rabbits, and muntjac, but also the success of fledgling birds, which often spend their first 24 hours post-fledgling in cover, but on the ground calling for food.

I accept that pet ownership is a personal choice, but its ecological impact is widely underestimated.

Likewise, disturbance in the wider countryside is often overlooked – especially the harm caused to **ground-nesting birds** and the dispersal of feeding flocks, both of which suffer when people are unaware how far that impact can travel from a footpath.

There is a myth in this country that, as nature lovers, our pets are only doing what comes naturally and therefore cannot be causing harm. **Twenty-six million cats and dogs are not natural**.

Safety
Inconvenient truth No 3:
Predator control.
Through years of disconnecting society from nature, we have created a dilemma about predator control, as we struggle to face the simple truth: we are part of nature and the apex predator in the UK. We are in a bind, not able to face the challenge of legal predator control.

Why do conservationists and gamekeepers, town and country, seem poles apart, when both groups of people want the same thing? The answer is often the ideological view that nothing must die. But this is nature; things die constantly. Are we playing God? Yes, but we are the apex predator, like it or not, and we have created this heavily populated and managed landscape.

I use a quote below from the *Guardian* newspaper: The environmental reporter for the *Guardian* discussing curlew conservation, 11 September 2025, quoting Wild Justice:

'The three main long-term issues that need to be addressed include intensive agriculture, where silage-making increases feeding opportunities for carrion crows and reduces the breeding success of curlews; the annual release of up to 60 million non-native pheasants and red-legged partridges, which sustain artificially-high numbers of predators and scavengers; and the illegal killing of birds of prey, including species such as goshawks, which would otherwise limit the populations of mesopredators and scavengers'.

So two out of the three main reasons for curlew decline (I accept the first one) are due to shooting, either from the release of too many birds, and the illegal killing of birds of prey especially goshawks. I do not condone any illegal killing of birds of prey and agree that too many birds are released for sport – but are these two factors really the most significant causes of the decline of the curlew? If you take the *Guardian* article literally, Wild Justice is saying two of the main problems are the shooting industry. Is the science there?

I would say there are four key causes of curlew decline. (1), yes, agreed, are **agricultural practices** (including silage production), followed by

(2) **disturbance** from people and dogs,

(3) increased **forestry**, and

(4) a reduction in **legal predator control**, i.e. fewer gamekeepers.

It is distracting to bring shooting into the argument. The phrase 'long term' keeps coming in, but we are here now in the short term. Whatever the population of goshawks we have, I am not sure they can keep the crow numbers down, especially with so many fat pigeons around, and goshawks' requirement for large individual territories. Even if I thought their numbers were being artificially kept low – which I don't.

Let me now bring this back to our garden, and some people may find this unpalatable, but a) I want to tell the truth, and b) I feel too much in conservation is being hidden from the public, in case they withdraw their funding.

The need to face facts

I control grey squirrels, rats (because grey squirrels and rats predate bird nests), carrion crows, and magpies. This does not harm their national or even local populations, and, like any countryman, I absolutely accept them as part of our fauna. However, during the nesting season, my garden is off limits.

In a twist of fate, as the songbird population builds up during the summer, we increasingly see sparrowhawks in the garden, a natural result of how prey controls predator numbers. I am the sparrowhawk's guardian too. I am not opposed to **birds of prey** – I am simply making a point.

Our natural world is being destroyed, Rome burns, and too often the truth goes untold. We are led to believe that people living and working in the countryside, and, God forbid, those who practise field sports, are the villains. If we left everything alone, the world would automatically be better, and biodiversity would flourish, the argument goes.

But we no longer live in a natural world – the UK has over 260,000 miles of roads and over 28 million homes. Nature has to work around this, all the fences, chemicals, pollution, agriculture, water abstraction and the sheer weight and waste of seventy million humans. I like to think I have maximised our garden for biodiversity and abundance, and in the context of the modern world on this small island, I sometimes have to play God.

Habitat can play a key role in mitigating the potential predators. Be a little more relaxed with tidiness, take a looser approach, be less meticulous, more easygoing, more unkempt, and less fastidious. Who is your judge, your neighbour, or yourself?

Much of the herbaceous plants' and wildflowers' withered stems I leave over winter – they hold gleanings for the goldfinches and green finches – and some I will stuff into the hedge.

I was cutting back a hedge that had grown leggy, while elderflowers thrusting too quickly through the beech and privet had created gaps. I know, I am now being fastidious – but after all, a well-kept hedge signals safety, a haven for countless small creatures seeking cover, even if only to cross from one side of the garden to the other.

As I worked, I noticed the ground was pocked with fresh molehills. The dry summer had drawn them here, where shaded soil offered refuge for worms and sanctuary for the moles themselves. Clearing away the clippings, I left small stacks of wood and leaves along the hedge bottom.

Flowers attract summer insects, but make sure to leave some areas for hibernation and overwintering larvae.

Different motivations frequently cloud conservation debates, with participants often talking past one another or deliberately obscuring their true agendas. I recently listened to a discussion on the banning of trail hunting in which a proponent of the ban asked why anyone would choose to mount a horse and follow an artificial scent with hounds. If the question was genuinely aimed at understanding motivation, it was spot on. If, as it appeared, it was an exaggerated rhetorical device, then it missed the point entirely: that trail hunting, for its participants, represents a cultural way of life rather than a logical exercise to be deconstructed.

Understanding people by their motivation, not necessarily their actions, can help bring parties together. So let me explore my love of birds, which has informed my motivation for writing this book:

How it all began for me: keeping hens

Chickens gave me my first love of birds. I was about eight when I was gifted an entire day off from primary school to watch our new garden chicken arrivals. 'You'll learn more than being at school,' my mother said, as she phoned the headmaster and explained my absence.

I lifted the wooden trap door to the battered second-hand hen house and stood back in anticipation. Little did the chickens know I would have happily waited all day to see them hesitantly take their first awkward plunge down the wooden ramp to their new world. First out was Chanterelle.

He was the poster boy cockerel, the enblazoned Coq Sportif of the French rugby shirt.

Crowning his head was a massive, blood-infused fleshy comb, matched by a similar pair of red wattles framing either side of his beak. Around his intense orange eyes was a perfect ring of red flesh flecked with white dots – and that was just his face. Yet it was his strut I noticed first. Each stride sent a pulsating rhythm down through the glossy green hackles of his neck, then down further to the larger saddle feathers draped about his rump. Before my gaze could settle, it lingered on the massive arc of a tail, the long, curved feathers defying gravity for a foot before drooping gracefully to the ground. And oh, how he adored himself: his girls called from the shadows, ushered under his command to watch him jive across the yard.

There were two speckled hens, certainly past their prime, two very old Brahmas, almost bigger than Chanterelle, certainly rounder. Bringing up the rear were two point-of-lay light Sussex hens: a ragtag flock bought in the pub. Life would never be quite the same again. My father was convinced that to maximise egg capacity, they required a hot meal every day. Returning from primary school each day, I was greeted by the smell of the chicken pot simmering on the Rayburn: potato and apple peelings, bread crusts and any leftovers were mixed with Layers' Mash into a crude paste, which, to be fair, the chickens loved, although I always thought my father was trying to make the mash go further and save money.

I don't think the Brahmas ever laid a single egg; the speckled Marans, to be generous, were sporadic (although they laid a beautiful, rich, dark chocolate egg), so it was left to the two Light Sussex hens to lay for six, which was never going to happen. But they taught me the rudiments of husbandry, a respect for animals, and how to get inside the brain of your living subject. Before their arrival, I had enthusiastically weeded a neighbour's entire vegetable garden, then transplanted the weeds into the soon-to-be chicken run, eager for their eclectic tastes. I was not disappointed. (At this point, pity the farmed chicken that has a single, monotonous diet every day.)

Their favourite weed was simple grass, which was soon exhausted, to be followed by clover, shepherd's purse, and the tufted vetch I had carefully nurtured with much watering. Lastly, there were dandelions, until nothing was left except mint, which was entirely left alone. I have ever since planted mint in my chicken runs to maintain some greenery about the place. In a way, all this data was secondary to a wish to observe how they busied themselves in their own world, the chicken run.

I noted the gentle shutting of their eyes when they dipped their beaks into the water before throwing their heads backwards to allow gravity to quench their thirst. Chickens do drink a lot. My mother was right about my education. The first life lesson is to observe and watch, see the details, and read what an artist sees. My father, in the meantime, seemed aggrieved that the neighbour had not paid me for weeding his garden, feeling my generosity had been taken for granted. He did not understand my motivations, confirmed when he bought four goslings to disrupt my peaceful ark, sending poor old Chanterelle into an epic fit of all-day crowing, which brought the threat of having his neck wrung hanging over the garden.

Charlie Fox rendered the threat redundant a few days later when someone forgot to shut the chicken coop for the night, and a trail of bloodied chickens stretched all the way to the woods half a mile away. The goslings were never found. There were some raised voices about how the smell of the geese had been a magnet for the fox. 'Everyone knows that!' A more likely explanation was father coming home late from the pub and forgetting to shut the chicken door.

To satisfy my thirst for revenge, father said he would ask 'Ol' Harold' to come and sit with his gun all night and shoot the varmint. I'm not sure which frightened me most, 'Ol' Harold' or the fox, but the suggestion seemed an excellent proposal. I waited for him first to get over the flu, then Christmas, and so it went all the way to March, and planting out the spuds. Second lesson in life – if you want something done, do it yourself.

It was a further two years before I shot my first fox, in fact two together, as the last square of barley trembled with the inevitability of the ever-encroaching combine. A dash for freedom became a dash to death. The foxes failed to break for freedom, their demise, my smile, slung triumphantly over my handlebars, as I cycled six miles to a furrier in Reading to sell their skins. 'Sonny, these two are worthless; the coat has to go through a winter to have any value.' Halfway home, I dumped the poor bodies in a hedge. Lesson number three in life. Prep, plan, and know your subject.

Our replenishment of the first chickens was not much better, and it was a good example of 'You pay peanuts, expect monkeys.' The excitement built as I opened the hen house door next morning to see our new flock.

Father proudly announced that not only would these chickens lay for another two years, but we were doing them a favour, as the local chicken farmer always killed them after a year. Open the big door, nothing happened, so I went inside where the girls were all sitting on the straw. I picked one up and gently placed it outside on the ground. The poor animal's legs were so weak that it could not stand, and I was taught the subtle art of how to wring a chicken's neck. It also gave me an education on battery farming, the cramped quarters, a life standing on a metal grid, the endless life of peck thy neighbour.

And so the first stirrings of conservation crept into my consciousness, industrial farming, and the provenance of our food.

Another childhood pastime of the 1960s and 70s that fostered my early love of nature was collecting birds' eggs. By taking only a single egg from each nest, I convinced myself I was acting as a progressive conservationist should. This was a period of growing awareness about how agricultural chemicals were accumulating in the food chain, leading to the thinning of birds' eggshells – particularly among birds of prey – and coinciding with the publication of Rachel Carson's *Silent Spring*. As birds of prey declined, the demand – and presumably the value – of their eggs increased, and egg collectors quickly became *persona non grata*. It is hard to imagine that the total population of red kites in those days was less than 50 birds, constrained by a genetic bottleneck and the constant harassment of egg collectors.

Indeed, when in the late 1980s birds of prey were imported from Spain to be released into the Chilterns, this was a deliberate decision to improve genetic robustness. Still, the choice of sites was well-keepered estates to help shield the birds from egg collectors.

Of course no one should take any eggs from nests today. But that love of discovering a nest full of eggs endures to this day, and who knows if this book would have been written without those early days of foraging and hunting the hedgerows?

Ask anyone in conservation what motivates them, and you will get the real story.

PART SIX

Mayfly

MAKING A GARDEN WILDLIFE-FRIENDLY

In the past, my garden would have melted seamlessly into the wider countryside. It would have been of no ecological curiosity, demanding no explanation. It would have been simply part of a managed landscape. Not because the past was 'wilder', because the countryside was, in many respects, more managed in the past, but we worked with nature rather than against it. It was, quite simply, kinder.

Modern conservation thinking is too often trapped in a romantic idyll of Britain beneath some primordial wildwood. Plant more trees, we are told, and everything will be healed. Healed of what, exactly? And for whose benefit? This nostalgia masquerading as science conveniently sidesteps a far more relevant question: when was our bio-abundance and biodiversity at its greatest? Between the world wars in the last century, when farming was less intensive, chemical use was lower, and people still worked the land with intimacy rather than abstraction.

Instead, we commit two intellectual sleights of hand. First, we compare a Britain of a few million souls with one now approaching seventy million. Second, we lazily import Yellowstone as our control condition, as if the ecological rules of a sparsely inhabited American wilderness could be cut-and-pasted onto one of the most densely populated landscapes on earth. Release the wolves, we are told, and mesopredators will melt away, balance will be restored, and equilibrium will reign. It is a comforting fairy tale.

This is apples-and-pears ideology dressed up as ecological inevitability, born of a deep discomfort with an inconvenient truth. In the United Kingdom, whether we like it or not, man is the ultimate apex predator.

To deny that is not rewilding – it is abdication.

Why rewilding can't solve the problem

The UK is roughly 3,550 times more densely populated than Yellowstone when measured in people per square mile.

Yellowstone's very low density reflects its status as a protected wilderness area with very few year-round human residents and vast natural landscapes. In contrast, the UK is a highly populated country with dense urban and suburban settlement patterns.

Over 70% of our land is farmed, yet we persist in pretending that stepping away from land management is somehow the virtuous choice. I argue instead for regenerative farming within an actively managed landscape, including the uncomfortable but necessary acceptance that predator control has a role in maintaining balance.

The evidence is already written across our uplands: where management is abandoned, the spring chorus falls silent. Our once mighty wader populations of dunlin, redshank, golden plover, lapwing, snipe, and curlew all decline, followed by short-eared owls, hen harriers, meadow pipits, cuckoos, and merlin. **Doing nothing is not neutrality; it is a decision with consequences**. The uplands are our nurseries, our islands of safety, largely abandoned in the harshness of winter, as most of the birds move to lowland farms or the coast for survival.

And while I am pushing an agenda, our Atlantic climate favours grass so beloved by cows and sheep, creating a virtuous protein cycle of eat and manure. It produces national food without the harmful practices of carbon-releasing ploughing, food miles, or offsetting our carbon emissions out of sight, thousands of miles away. I am not advocating inflated sheep numbers, nor Texan-scale enclosures crammed with cattle, but a clear-eyed recognition of our natural capacity to produce sustainable grass, and to use it well.

Plant with purpose: encourage and help insects thrive, and the birds will benefit.

As you drift through the garden centre, the colours call out like sweets in jars – irresistible, fleeting. It's too easy to fall for the instant charm of blooms already peaked, a takeaway for the eyes – here today, gone tomorrow. Some wear the 'bee-friendly' badge yet offer little when bees first wake in spring and need it most. Plant with purpose. Choose flowers that truly nourish. And as for fruitless ornamentals – why settle for show alone? A tree that feeds bees and bears fruit gives much more in return.

Here are my top six early insect-friendly plants, carefully selected to provide the most significant boost in spring and early summer (from February to May), when pollinators need them most. Many birds who have fed at your bird table through the winter need insects and grubs for their young in early spring. For best results, plant them in sheltered spots that catch the morning sun, providing warmth and nectar as the insects begin their day. To add some glamour, I have focused on bees, but they are all-round insect attractors.

The magnificent six for spring
Crocus (but choose the right ones!)

Crocuses are among the best early spring plants for bees, especially bumblebee queens emerging from hibernation. However, not all species are equally helpful. You want early flowering crocus species, ideally those with orange or purple flowers, and nectar-rich.

One of the earliest to flower – often by late February – is *Crocus tommasinianus* or *Crocus vernus*, both open-faced varieties that serve their pollen generously. I grow them on a south-facing grassy slope I call my crocus bank. It's the first place I look each spring to catch the emerging bumble bees.

Avoid the large, overbred double varieties. They have less pollen and are often harder for the bees to access.

Pussy willow

This is one of the year's first quiet miracles – its soft, silken catkins catching the light before most trees have even stirred. This usually refers to the male catkins of goat willow (*Salix caprea*) and grey willow (*Salix cinerea*), which may be the only flowers available if the weather is poor. Therefore, when planting, choose male trees (with the yellow, pollen-rich catkins). Female trees bear greenish catkins and don't provide the same benefit.

Flowering from late winter into early spring, its golden catkins are rich in nectar and pollen, offering a vital lifeline to queen bumble bees waking from hibernation. But it's not just bees – recently arrived chiffchaffs and willow warblers also depend on this early bounty. Planted in a sunny, sheltered spot, pussy willow becomes a beacon for the season's first stirrings of life.

Pulmonaria
My next early insect-friendly plant is lungwort (*Pulmonaria*). This shade-tolerant plant, with its spotted leaves and two-toned flowers, is an early buffet for long-tongued bees and dark-edged flies. This year we had the common carder bee, the early bumblebee. Buff-tailed bumblebee and white-tailed bumblebee all feed on lungwort as it fills a vital gap between the crocus and pussy willow before the bulk of the spring flowers.

White dead-nettle
Often dismissed as a weed, the white dead-nettle (*Lamium album*) is a quiet hero of spring. Flowering early and generously, it offers nectar from late March

to May. Unlike its stinging cousin, it's easy to recognise and even easier to lift and replant – its shallow roots make it a gentle guest in any garden. I let it grow wherever it chooses – not just for the bees, but for its delicate white flowers, and as a reminder of spring. By summer, it retreats quietly back into the soil.

You are unlikely to find this in the garden centre, so treasure it if it grows in your garden. It is a plant of hedgerows and shady spots, perfect for wild places in the garden, but I find it equally at home in an herbaceous border. The white, hooded blooms are specially shaped for long-tongued bumble bees, such as white-tailed bees. Even on cold spring days, they produce a reliable nectar supply for many early insects.

Comfrey
Comfrey, especially the early blooming varieties, is a powerhouse for spring insects with its tubular blooms. It is a straightforward plant to grow from any snapped-off piece of its thick but weak tap roots – I let it grow wherever it pleases, if not bothering other plants. I then cut down the old flower stems to add to the compost heaps.

Technically a little later than spring, but I had to include borage as it is so easy to grow and a must for bees. Look after the bees, they will pollinate and the flowers and insects will follow.

Borage (a little later) (*Borago officinalis*)

Although not strictly 'spring', borage blooms soon after and continues to flower until the autum. Early insects love it, and I let it self-seed and come up each year across the vegetable garden. Apart from the nectar, the two-tone blue and mauve/pink colors make them a very visually distinct flower for bees to identify. And then, of course, you can pick the flowers for drinks or to colour your salads.

Two large blocks of perennial wildflowers support a diverse array of insects, which in turn attract birds, frogs, and grass snakes. A tapestry of flowers begins in February, with white snowdrops, before moving on to a palette of yellow, featuring crocuses, celandines, buttercups, and dandelions. Next, we enter the red campion and ragged robin phase before the blues of bluebells, and the white frothiness of cow parsley. The spring then gives way to the first summer purples of knapweed and scabious bloom before the mauve marjoram. I do weed out stinging nettles and docks. Marjoram's beauty lies in its naturalness, which draws in wildlife from all around – but I am missing something. My mind travels back to childhood.

I am in a field of spring barley, aged around ten, and take pity on a skylark which appears to have a broken wing. I am clueless to its sham. I chase it, tripping, falling among the young barley and weeds before the mass applications of hormone herbicides. A final lunge, and I have the bird in my hand – a triumph! Grazed with scratched knees, I hurry home, having come of age with such a prize, and carefully place it in a cage among the guinea pigs and a single canary-coloured budgerigar. I am reading Gerald Durrell – embarking on my own *My Family and Other Animals*. The 'other animals' are doing well. I am then Billy Casper in *Kes*, and I cannot wait to relay my capture to my mother. Children's dreams get shattered, and my mother explained the error of my ways and how the skylark was only trying to lure me away from her nest. I released the bird, and sure enough, she fluttered strongly into the sky, back to whence she came. But I never forgot that episode and the field of barley with its radiant corn marigolds, their glaucous smooth leaves, and on the brow of the hill the red poppies, some with their heads bending shyly down like Princess Diana, others open and alive bright faces in the barley.

I already have a wildflower meadow, but I wanted the corn marigolds, poppies, chamomile, and cornflowers of the arable field – their beauty highlighted and enhanced by the ephemerality of it all so I dug up a herbaceous border cursed with bindweed, which drove its white maggot roots into every crevice of the phlox, daisy, sedum, delphinium, and peony root balls – and cast them aside. Then I had to weed the newly emergent bindweed roots that regrew from just inch-long pieces of broken root, again and again.

Finally, I had a seedbed, a fine tilth to broadcast my arable weeds. This was the middle of March, and within a month, the dry spring meant I only had small wisps of yes, more bindweed, and the odd thistle to show appreciation for my super-worked tilth. I had to resort to watering, but bit by bit, a green washed over the soil if you got down on your hands and knees in the evening.

By the beginning of June, the first white chamomile flowers appeared, with spots of yellow marigolds, and by the end of the month, the blue cornflowers and red poppies demanded attention from every passerby. Goldfinches quickly found the cornflower seeds, and hedge sparrows and wrens worked their way through the stems. Bees and hoverflies favoured the poppies and chamomile, while the cornflowers and corn marigolds attracted smaller butterflies, including common blue and small copper. But most of all, it drew me in and took me back to that childhood barley field with the skylark who took me for a ride, and taught me that sometimes things aren't what they seem, and all that glitters is not gold.

In September, on the other side of the astronomical coin, the magic and charm of discovering a few bright corn marigolds remain with the odd azure blue of a late cornflower. The riot is over, and in the silence, these are shy mementos hidden in the dried stems of summer glory gone.

Great tit

GROW YOUR OWN
BIRDSEED

Plant with purpose, grow your own bird seed.

'A weed,' you say. 'Beware!' And yes, left to its own devices, it will happily invade your lawn. But let's see it for the joy it brings. Take the **foxglove**: it sits quietly in its first year, a humble rosette of leaves, unassuming, just waiting. Then, in its second year, it rises – a wild, untamed beauty – its spiny, bright green stems stretching upwards to equally spiky egg-shaped mauve flowering bracts. At this point not just its beauty but its generosity comes to light.

These tiny mauve flowers enrich your garden in clustered bands, enticing the bees and butterflies first before, later in the year, the twinkly, twittering flocks of goldfinches seek out the prickly seedheads.

Wrapped around the stem, the leaves form a verdant cup, collecting water, which seems to defy evaporation, perfectly pitched above the ground. Like all good 'weeds,' they are easy to grow, often referred to as a plant of 'waste grounds', a desultory, demeaning term for both the habitat and the plant, once banished to the outer edges of cultivation. What they really like is disturbed soil, where the seeds can become established. They scatter themselves across your gravel pathways and flowerbeds, tolerating drought and dry conditions with their strong, radiating root system. But before I scare you away, they are easy to pull out and readily take to transplanting in the right place. Across the garden, we have four clumps that attract the goldfinches.

Easy-growing **teasels** will be at home in most places, but they keep their nectar protected deep inside the flower. As a result, they have developed close relationships with long-tongued insects, especially bumble bees, moths, and butterflies.

Unusually, and unlike foxgloves, they flower from the centre of the flower head outward. Their unique blooming pattern starts with a ring of tiny flowers forming around the middle of the cylindrical flower head. Over time, the flowers gradually expand upward and downward, creating a distinctive two-tone appearance as different sections bloom at various stages.

Buff-tailed, white-tailed, garden, and red-tailed (*Bombus*) bumble bees, with their relatively long tongues, take advantage of the long flowering season and the sizeable conical landing pad where they forage alongside similarly long-tongued butterflies, especially large whites, peacocks, brimstones, and red admirals.

These are tall plants, with the flowers typically held head height or higher, helping us to observe their many followers. We associate the soft yellow brimstone butterfly with spring, primrose, daffodils, and dandelions. But here in late summer, you get a second brood, a second chance to feast on the fresh buttery colours, feeding intensely on the rich nectar to build up reserves for hibernation. We will not see them again before they awaken on some mild February day next year, signalling spring long before the first swallow or, if you're fortunate, the cuckoo call.

No other bird shares a bond with a teasel like the goldfinch. With their long pointy beaks, they can reach the rich seeds buried deep in the now brown seedheads, which others would struggle to access. I believe these 'buried' seeds also keep the food available longer into the winter, although they are ripe by the end of September. Many of you reading will buy similar-sized 'niger' seeds, which goldfinch also love, but they will just as happily flock noisily to the rich, fat, and protein-rich teasel seeds. Grow your natural birdseed.

With an abundance of food all winter, our goldfinches hang around the garden all year round, always together in their cheerful way. For nests, they choose the crook of a hazel, apple, lilac, or creeper around the house, at a favoured height of between ten and twenty feet, with multiple broods from April through to late August. This small flock or 'charm' (their collective name) builds up to over twenty by late summer.

In my garden they nest in a climbing hydrangea. They also nest in the honeysuckle, conveniently constructed just below our bedroom window, occasionally with an unusual clutch of five eggs against the usual four. They have mesmerised me since boyhood.

Goldfinches have one other plant relationship in the garden – **Jerusalem artichokes**. They strip material from the stems, weaving it together with horsehair and wool from the fields, creating a strong nest structure for such a small bird. These carefully crafted nursery cups are still visible long after the leaves have fallen, deep into January, braving it against the winter winds, a distant summer memory.

For plant lovers, with Jerusalem artichokes you have a special towering structure and architectural seedheads in the winter. But for me, the joy is the bees when those light mauve bands of flowers first open in July with the later promise of brimstones and goldfinches to come.

Another 'grow your own bird seed' is the common **sunflower**. Here you are focusing especially on great tits and coal tits, which will pick the seeds directly from the old seed heads, although a whole host of birds will pick on any seed falling to the ground.

Late August to early September, the first sunflower heads begin to droop as the old flowers, now heavy with seed, weigh them down. Once the yellow papery calex drops to the ground, it exposes the black nutritious seeds. Sunflowers are scattered randomly across the garden, and soon there is a flurry of activity as both coal and great tits acrobatically hang under these sagging flowers. Here is evolution in action, as only these two birds have a beak long enough to pick the sunflower seeds out, or at least I have never encountered any other members of the titmouse feeding in this way.

There is a parallel delight here with growing your own vegetables, and you are providing a more natural way to feed the birds.

POWER OF A
COMPOST HEAP

One of my finest wildlife gardening achievements is the nurturing of grass snakes *Natrix helvetica* in my compost heap. These fascinating creatures always try to avoid humans and prefer to slip away unnoticed. Chances are, you've already been near one without realising it. Unless you actively look for them, they will probably pass you by.

Just as mesmerising as anything you might see on TV, a three-foot-long female grass snake moves across the land with the fluidity of a fish in water. Her graceful, curved form and commanding beauty will stop you in your tracks, captivated by her poise, amazed by her grace and elegance. You don't need to travel abroad to see this magnificent creature – it lives wild right here in the UK. The national population is estimated to be around 320,000 individuals, although the figure is somewhat uncertain. What is clear, however, is that local habitat restoration can boost their numbers, and this is where we can all help – starting in our own gardens.

No other animal in Britain wears such a remarkable palette of muted greens, shifting from a variable light olive-brown through shades of green tinged with blue undertones to near black, set against a lighter pale underside. You, the danger, the predator, find your eyes subtly diverted from the head and piercing gaze by the striking yellow neckband – nature's perfect distraction.

These masters of camouflage share their cloaks of green with only a select few: the green woodpecker, another ground hunter, some grasshoppers and crickets, and, of course, their favourite prey – frogs, all perfectly adapted to their world.

Our paths rarely cross, and it's no wonder. However, if I've sparked your interest even a little, maybe piqued your curiosity, then as gardeners, we have a unique opportunity to support these remarkable wonders of the British countryside.

Being semi-aquatic and with a primary diet of frogs, toads, and newts, the best way to attract grass snakes is to create a sheltered, easily accessible, well-vegetated pond. You want the perfect environment for the snakes and their prey, a sign of a healthy and diverse ecosystem.

But rather than ponds, I'd like to focus on your compost pile. Long before I saw a grass snake in our garden, I would occasionally find their eggs in the compost heap. I think I have now perfected the ultimate compost management strategy for grass snakes. I knew I must be doing something right when, in December 2019, I uncovered the remains of 89 hatched grass snake eggs. The excitement here was the sheer number. As all the books say, grass snakes typically lay 20 to 30 eggs, so this could have been three snakes sharing my compost nursery, a super creche unknown to the world except the snakes and me.

Even more remarkable was that all 89 looked like they had successfully survived incubation and escaped to the outside world, meaning the physical environment must have been spot-on. When fresh, the eggs are white or creamy, but after nine months, these leathery shells, about the size of a grape with their insides sucked out, are stained a dirty cream colour. Many eggs are found stuck together, and their proximity to each other is thought to stimulate hatching synchronisation, as they feel the vibrations and hear faint noises from their siblings. I examined the exact position of each egg within the compost heap, and a recurring theme emerged.

All the eggs were laid at the base of the pile, where dried leaves met the season's first fresh cut of grass. Since they depend on the warmth from the decomposing grass, this suggests they are laid early in the season – likely around mid-May – which aligns with me finding the young in early August. We marvel at the lifecycle of turtles burying their eggs in a tropical sandy beach; these eggs are also soft-shelled and of a very similar composition, except they are buried in compost heaps, in your very own garden!

Each year, I scatter dried beech leaves at ground level – a base, a foundation – before covering them with freshly cut grass. The grass must be fresh, for it's the moisture that sparks the chemical reaction that generates heat. Yet another reason I still find myself mowing in May!

The eggs are consistently laid near the edges of the compost, where physical access is more straightforward and there is likely more oxygen available through the slatted wooden pallets. I've previously encountered snakes trapped in wire and nylon netting, so avoiding those materials is probably best. The pallets also provide some protection from foxes and badgers, but the weather likely plays a significant role in success or failure. It is well-documented that cooler summers can delay hatching by several weeks and, if it is too cold, the eggs may perish entirely. Compost gurus now suggest adding solid sides to increase the heat of the materials, encouraging faster decay.

Other considerations
Management
I maintain two compost heaps, alternating between them so that the older one is emptied by the end of the year, usually by December, while the other is filled during the summer. This approach minimises disturbance.

A word on the benefits of composting. Although compost has fewer nutrients than synthetic fertilisers, this natural process allows plants to absorb moisture and nutrients more effectively, making them stronger through the presence of beneficial microbes and bacteria. These mycorrhizal fungi produce a vast web of underground mycelia, which allows the plants to reach a wider area of soil. In return, they exude carbohydrates and lipids to feed the fungi. Fertilisers give the plants a 'sugar rush,' a quick fix, which means they stop provisioning the fungi, and so the soil becomes poorer.

As Merlin Sheldrake writes in his book *Entangled Life:*

'How fungi make our worlds, change our minds, and shape our futures'

We merely give them a helping hand and all the other wildlife in the garden – they do the rest.

Your compost heap is helping you free your garden from chemicals

Compost also serves as a mulch, reducing leaching and suppressing weeds. Remember the moles under the hedge I wrote about earlier – they had found sanctuary there in the hot, dry summer to feed on the worms, because the natural layers of compost built up over many years have given the soil resilience to drought.

Untidiness

Back to the snakes, and it is important to provide some cover around the compost heaps – here, I let the grass grow naturally long. An old, corrugated iron sheet warms the soil underneath – the perfect shelter for the snakes to raise their body temperature to a hunting level. From here, a corridor of unmown grass and wildflower turf leads all the way to the pond, which, in equal terms, provides shelter for the young toadlets, froglets, and baby newts. You now have the perfect ecosystem for a nest of eggs and, crucially, you ensure that food is available for the young.

Aspect

Both my compost heaps sit in a sheltered, south-facing spot, with a large tree and a fence providing protection to the north and east. Warmth is essential for the snakes' development. The heaps have no floor, only bare earth, allowing excess moisture to drain away and enabling microbes, worms, and a host of other small creatures to move freely in and out.

Observations

Snakes are not the easiest creatures to watch. While nature is often best observed by sitting quietly and letting it unfold before you, this may involve a long wait. My usual sightings are enabled as follows on warm days:

1. React to any disturbance in the pond and approach cautiously. Remember that your feet make vibrations, and your body casts shadows. The snakes usually lie submerged, with just their heads protruding at an angle, making them hard to see among the floating and emergent weeds.

2. Listen out for a soft, continuous rustle in dead leaves somewhere sheltered where the snake has been sunbathing. As you become better acquainted with the wildlife in your garden, these little things become second nature.

3. Patches of wildflowers and long grass are a magnet to grass snakes, and if you mow patches between them, you may sometimes see a snake crossing from one habitat to another.

And that's just the grass snakes!

Thrush with snail

EPILOGUE:
why I wrote this book

Like most diurnal creatures, we sharpen our inner senses in the dark, especially our hearing, and I wanted to be the first feet to tread this blank canvas an hour before dawn, before the birds rise to claim it as their own. They sing:

'I am here. This is my territory. Hear me sing – strong, clear, alive. If your heart stirs, come closer and be my mate. But if you are a rival, turn back now. Do not cross this boundary. My song carries farther in the cold, crisp air, calling you down from the heavens or drawing you out from the undergrowth. Either way, this is my land.'

The duller the bird, the sweeter the song. Where song is the primary weapon in sexual rivalry, plumage tends to be plain. Conversely, where colours blaze and courtship dances dazzle, the song often falters. Think of the drab yet exquisite nightingale versus the striking but croaking blackcock. Nature, it seems, rarely grants both beauty and song.

Like our good health, we rarely consider our ears until deafness interrupts. Helen Keller, who was both deaf and blind, famously said:

'Blindness cuts us off from things, but deafness cuts us off from people.'

Some argue that losing hearing is the greater loss, as it severs us from conversation and connection, making it harder to engage with others and the world around us. But today, we seem to have a diminishing ability to observe, yet it's free and open to everyone.

The English countryside has been immortalised from Constable paintings to Wedgwood Pottery, but who is noting the change in the soundscape?

Unravelling the dawn chorus

Many people consider the song of the cuckoo, chiffchaff, great tit, or song thrush to be their favourite sound of spring. The blackbird remains my favourite, whether in the early morning or the soft light of evening. They sing as we sing, with notes and rhythm, but there are also the ordinary bird voices: welcome voices, like the cheerful chatter of house martins fussing under the eaves.

Perhaps if I lived on the moors or on an ancient floodplain, my favourite would be different – a bubbling curlew or a dancing lapwing. But today, one day in May, we will discover everything natural in my garden in Wiltshire, from dawn to dusk, and everything in between.

What can you hear? Every rustle, hum, chirp, and whisper offers a message if you are willing to listen. And aim to convey how you too can make your garden super abundant with wildlife.

People often struggle to identify common animals and plants despite seeing them with their own eyes. Yet the sounds of creatures are all around us – we don't even have to look up – and it's an entire world that passes by so many.

Each moment brings its unique blend of sounds, helping us notice how the natural soundscape evolves. There's often more to hear than we first realise – it's an opportunity to pause, listen, and take in what's happening around us.

Who will be the first bird to enter the stage? We will most likely hear the robin, and then, after a slight interval, perhaps a song thrush or blackbird. These 'songbirds', called Passeriformes, comprise many species worldwide, with a broad representation in Wiltshire, England, including sparrows, finches, robins, thrushes, pipits, wagtails, warblers, buntings, swallows, martins, larks, starlings, and treecreepers. But who knows what we will hear on 6 May? We could just as easily be gatecrashed by a cock pheasant, carrion crow, or encounter the screech of a late-hunting barn owl.

For centuries, literature has been inspired by the songs of skylarks, nightingales, and cuckoos – a testament to the beauty and familiarity of their time. Though these birds are not as common today, there is still much to celebrate – seventeen hours, and we will know the answer.

We live in the middle of chalk stream catchments of the Hampshire Avon, which rises here in Wiltshire, to the south at All Cannings, and the River Kennet to our north, flowing east to meet the River Thames in Berkshire. Knowing what to expect in a locale helps identify species.

The richness of nature

We regularly record over fifty bird species in the garden, with nearly twenty nesting each year, so we have a good base to work with. Being only a paddock away from the river Kennet helps the mix of garden, water, farmland, and woodland birds. On a warmish last day of February, a dunnock was tuning a fitful, hurried burst of sound, and across the field, a song thrush was getting into full stride. They are preparing and planning for the full-on orchestra later in the year. A few silent midges are bouncing in the light air, and one buff-tailed bumblebee is humming as it bumbles around the purple crocuses – the world is waking up.

The mature trees attract birds to the garden. Years of enduring frost, scorching sun, heavy rains, and creeping fungi have transformed their trunks into miniature ecosystems. Vertical and horizontal fissures and ribbed cracks shelter countless insects, their eggs and larvae tucked behind lichen crusts and soft mounds of moss. Today, nuthatches, woodpeckers, and tree creepers scurry up and down the bark, while the titmouse family flits and twists among the finer outer branches to find a morsel. A goldcrest launches itself forward, snatching an invisible midge from the air. The trees bring them to me, a vertical landscape trebling the size of the garden.

The dawn chorus peaks from late April to early May, with the arrival of summer migrants swelling the ranks of our resident birds, all jostling for territory. How often do you hear the first swallow before seeing one, and how many of us have truly seen a cuckoo?

The sounds of spring are woven into my childhood, bringing me to life again each year, without anyone else's help, assistance, or influence. It is an intimate recognition of self, an unspoken truth.

I make that discovery – hearing, tasting, smelling, or seeing something – that thread connecting me to last year and the year before, stretching back in time. A safe return to the now.

What will be the first insect we hear as the sun climbs in the sky? Probably a honeybee or bumblebee, which, along with hoverflies, fly during cooler temperatures. We are a little early in the year to hear the rustle of a dragonfly or damselfly wing. Have you ever listened to the rustle of a toad on dry leaves or a grass snake through the herbage? They are distinct, but most untrained ears would not register a need to stop and look a little carefully around your feet. Once our ears pick up a sound, our instinct is to bring it into our vision, reach for the binoculars, or turn on the light. Other creatures might tilt their heads to listen more effectively or lift their snouts to sniff for identification. Today, we will tilt our heads a little more.

In his preface for *Our favourite Songbirds* in 1897, Charles Dixon wrote, 'The music of the fields and woodlands is one of the most gratifying pleasures of the country. But the vast number of people to whom the songs of birds are a constant source of delight know very few of the singers' identities, even if familiar enough with many of the songs, and are practically ignorant of their habits and economy.'

As true today as over a hundred years ago. In this little book, we will listen to their songs while also taking a closer look at some of their behaviours, which are often a key to identification.

A 17-hour experiment

The garden in May is a feast for the imagination. But to share something you love – a song, which by its very nature is an expression of emotions too vast to put into words – is the icing on the cake. It will build from perhaps a lone robin in the dark to a crescendo of birds, before tailing off, cueing over to the insect ensemble, a melodic passing by an invisible conductor whispering in the air, who later in the day passes back to the birds in their open-air theatre.

It will be a unique seventeen-hour opportunity to observe and record a wide range of activity. Sharing these observations, especially birdsong – an instinctive form of communication – is rewarding.

Urbanisation, climate change, and rapidly evolving agricultural practices all accelerate changes in biodiversity and fauna. These shifts typically create a situation where some species thrive while others struggle, thereby reducing species diversity. The 'winners' – the more adaptable species – tend to become more abundant, outcompeting those less equipped to survive in the changing environment or simply predating them. Today, we witness the 'winners' – an environment where wood pigeons thrive and populations of mesopredators, including foxes, badgers, squirrels, and crows, are rising. In addition, the presence of 70 million humans alongside an estimated 13 million dogs and 11 million cats in the

UK increases the 'losers'. We are forced to draw a new line in the sand – a reduced bio-abundance, marking a quieter countryside. This is why gardens increasingly play a crucial role in holding the line and providing a refuge for wildlife. However, they can only mitigate the impact to a limited extent, and our farmland birds and waders continue to decline. My childhood memories of abundant birdsong may have gone forever, but as a minimum, we should preserve what is left.

My garden is a leftover pocket of life – and that's part of why I invite you to read this book. We need more such places.

The best environment we can make

Earlier in the year: gorse

Back in March, I waited for the first spring day to arrive, bringing an unmistakable golden blaze – a coconut-sweet scent drifting on the warming air, like sunshine you can smell, arising from yellow, pea-like blooms so vivid they seem to define the essence of colour itself.

A scrubby plant of heath and moorland and, here in Wiltshire, the sheep-dotted downs, this unloved gorse, is too unruly for any garden centre, too damn spiky for any gardener.

Like a wild animal, undomesticated and prickly, it does its own thing.

'A touch of the untamed' carries certain benefits. Hidden deep within its prickly fortress are food, shelter, and – most crucially in today's environment – protection from nest predation. Gorse may be wild and unyielding, but it offers a sanctuary for birds, insects, and small mammals that few predators can reach. A rare refuge from disturbance by people and their pets.

These 'islands' of gorse thickets support nesting linnets, whitethroats, and yellowhammers – all farmland birds whose numbers have plummeted with more intensive agriculture. And, in an increasingly fragmented landscape, the less common Dartford warblers and stonechats.

Despite the wild beauty of gorse and its role in supporting nature, you're probably still not convinced about incorporating it into your garden, despite its sweet fragrance. And, of course, your garden may not be the preferred habitat of farmland birds anyway.

But it is a sure-fire way of helping one little garden bird.

After spending the winter entertaining you and benefiting from your generosity at the bird table, long-tailed tits may vanish in the spring, unable to nest nearby and unlikely to return until the following winter.

Many of us are good at putting up nest boxes, and their success comes from providing the right habitat for hole-nesting birds and offering protection from predators. But long-tailed tits don't nest in holes. Instead, they create their own remarkable domed nests with an entrance hole woven from thousands of pieces of moss, lichen, and animal hair. Inside, the nest is lined with soft feathers, while outside, their home is camouflaged with local lichen.

They are vulnerable, but these endearing birds have one more trick up their sleeves: they nearly always nest in the thorniest, densest bushes they can find at about head height or a little lower. In the garden, I have found them nesting in blackthorn (*Prunus spinosa*), hawthorn (*Crataegus monogyna*), and crown of thorns (*Euphorbia milii*).

However, in the wider countryside, they find prickly gorse an even more suitable habitat. So feed the birds in the winter and help them find a safe place to nest in the spring with *Ulex Europaeus* – common gorse. Next to a crown-of-thorns bush, I have created the perfect blend of prickliness and shelter. Three gorse bushes, with their dense, spiky protection, a wild rose, and teasels all contribute to extra layers of security. The mature trees overhead offer the added benefit of cover and shade.

It's not difficult – I can maintain the dense shape these little birds love by pruning the gorse each autumn with simple shears or a hedge trimmer. It works. A pair of long-tailed tits built their nest so deep within the gorse that I can only just make out a carefully woven mass of moss and lichen, deep in the shadows. But we'll see and hear them today as they flit through the trees, hurrying back with food for their young.

A Ukrainian woman working in a British garden recently spoke about the differences between gardens here and back home. She said Ukrainians aim for bold splashes of colour – sunflowers, peonies, roses. Here, she's learning to blend more subtle tones into the landscape, guided by a lighter human touch, striving for an unseen hand. The birdsong in Wiltshire is much the same – you couldn't compose it yet, like the garden, it somehow all comes together.

Acknowledgements

I was kept company all day by two dedicated heroes.

David White, Wildlife Photographer - who had to suffer my presence for 17 hours on 6 May.

Alex Byng Cameraman - who had to also suffer my presence for 17 hours.

References

Entangled Life Merlin Sheldrake

Silent Spring Rachel Carson

Merlin Bird ID app
Free, instant bird identification help and guide for thousands of birds – Identify the birds you see and hear.
https://merlin.allaboutbirds.org

The Woodland Trust
Abigail Bunker, Woodland Trust director of conservation
https://www.woodlandtrust.org.uk

British Trust for Ornithology (BTO)
https://www.bto.org/our-science/publications/birdtrends

RSPB https://www.rspb.org.uk

Manchester Guardian

Conservation Communication
www.conservationcommunication.com

Index

Further reading from
Merlin Unwin Books

Wild Flowers of Britain *Margaret Erskine Wilson*

Woodland Wild Flowers *Alan Waterman*

Cuckoo Calls the Year *Pete Stroh*

Eat Your Weeds *Julie Bruton-Seal & Matthew Seal*

Hedgerow Medicine *Julie Bruton-Seal & Matthew Seal*

Wayside Medicine *Julie Bruton-Seal & Matthew Seal*

Wild World *Richard Barrett*

A Murmuration of Starlings *Steve Palin*

Wild Enthusiasm *Steve Wright*

To Everything a Season *Charles Moseley*

My Wood *Stephen Dalton*

Land's End to John O'Groats *Helen Shaw*

Wildlife of the Pennine Hills *Doug Kennedy*

Mushrooming Without Fear *Alexander Schwab*

Pocket Guide to Essential Knots *Peter Owen*

Full details
www.merlinunwin.co.uk